# ENCYCLOPAEDIA OF WOMEN IN SOUTH ASIA (BANGLADESH)

# ENCYCLOPAEDIA
# OF
# WOMEN IN SOUTH ASIA

*(In 8 Volumes)*

## Bangladesh

## (Volume 3)

*Editors :*

**Sangh Mittra, Bachchan Kumar**

**KALPAZ PUBLICATIONS**

**Delhi-110052**

Encyclopaedia of Women in South Asia (*Bangladesh*)
*(International Studies, Women)*

Rs. 7000 (Set)

ISBN: 81-7835-187-0 (Set)
ISBN: 81-7835-190-0 (Vol. 3)



Published in 2004 in India by
Kalpaz Publications,
C-30, Satyawati Nagar, Delhi-110052
E-mail : Kalpaz@hotmail.com

*Laser Typesetting at* : Shree Vaishnavi Creations, Delhi
*Printed at* : Mehra Offset Press, Delhi

# Contents

# 1

# Historical Background, Geography and People

## Location and Area

Bangladesh is located at the eastern end of the Indo-Gangetic plain in Southern Asia. It extends 767 km (477 mi) SSE to NNW and 429 km (267mi) ENE to WSW. It has a total land area of 142,776 sq km 55,126 sq mi).

Bangladesh's total international land boundary of 2,816 km (1,750 mi) is shared with two countries : India (2,583 km, 1,605 mi) and Burma (233 km, 145 mi). The Indo-Bangladesh boundary line was determined by the Radcliffe Award at the time of the partition of the Indian Empire into India and Pakistan in 1947. The border was ratified by the Bangladesh legislature in 1974. The Burma-Bangladesh border was fixed in 1937 at the time of the separation of Burma from India.

The capital is Decca with a 1974 population of 1,679,572. The other major urban centres are Chittagong (1,000,000), Khulna (530,000) and Narayanganj (270,680).

Topographically, Bangladesh may be divided into the vast alluvial plain comprising most of the country and the small Chittagong Hill Tracts in the extreme southeast. The Bengal plain, also known as the Lower Indo-Gangetic Plain, is a large delta, in fact, the largest delta in the world. The Chittagong Hill Tracts constitute roughly one-sixth of the country. They form a minor hill system with its greatest elevation at Keokradong (1,229 metres, 4,034 ft). Toward the east they form a series of parallel hill chains, while toward the west they slope gradually into a small, coastal plain.

Bangladesh has one of the most complex river systems in the world forming an interlacing grid. The three principal rivers of this network are : the Ganges (known as Padma in Bangladesh), the Brahmaputra (known as Jamuna in Bangladesh), and the Meghna.

**Weather**

Bangladesh has a tropical climate governed by the monsoons. Though it is comparatively temperate and equable, there are marked seasonal variations. The three main seasons are a hot, summer season from March to June, a cooler but still warm and humid monsoon season from June through September and a cool, dry, winter season from October to February. January is the coolest month and April and May the hottest.

The average temperatures range from 7°C (45°F) in January to 31°C (88°F) in August and 32°C (90°F) in May. Temperatures up to 40.6°C (105°F) have been occasionally recorded. Daily temperature changes are moderate.

**Population**

The population of Bangladesh in 1980 was 89,284,000 based on the last official census held in 1974 when the population was 71,479,071. Bangladesh ranks eighth in the world in size of population. The annual rate of population growth is estimated at 2.7 per cent based on an annual birthrate of 49.5 per 1,000. The population is expected to reach 146 million by the year 2000.

Bangladesh is the second most densely populated nation in the world after Singapore. The population density in 1974 was 533 per sq km (1,380 per sq mi) for the country as a whole. If the arable and populated areas are considered separately, the density rises to over 1,550 per sq km (4,014 per sq mi). At the 1974 census males numbered 37,017,740 and females 34,407,331. The resulting male/female ratio was 51.86 :48.14.

**Ethnic Composition**

Bangladesh is noted for the remarkable ethnic homogeneity of its population. Over 98 per cent of its people are Bengalees (also spelt Bengalis). The remaining two per cent is accounted for by Biharis and tribals. The term Bihari designates non-Bengali, Urdu-speaking Muslims who fled to Bangladesh from eastern India in 1947. The tribals live mainly in the Chittagong Hill Tracts. The largest of these are the Chakmas, the Marmas, the Tipperas and the Moros. The tribals are racially distinct from the Bengalees. Their facial features and language are closer to the Burmese.

**Languages**

Bangla, or Bengali, is the official language of Bangladesh. Bangalees identify themselves with their national language very closely. Bangla has a rich literature; at least two Bangla writers are well known in the West : Nobel Laureate Rabindranath Tagore and Kazi Nazrul Islam.

English remains the language of the modern sector. But its cultural use seems to have crested and is beginning to decline. The availability of typewriters with Bangla script has hastened the displacement of English by the national language.

**Religions**

Bangladesh is also remarkably homogeneous in religious affiliations. Nearly 90 per cent of the people are Muslims, making Bangladesh the second largest Islamic country in the world, after Indonesia. Although loyalty to Islam is deep-rooted, the content and social structure of Islam have been influenced by Hinduism,. Although Islam does not recognize caste, Bengali Muslim society is divided into three groups: ashraf (better class), ajlaf (lower class) and arzal lowest class. Each group is further divided into smaller groups. In many cases, beliefs and observances in rural areas tend to conflict with those of orthodox Islam. Most Muslims belong to the Sunnsect.

The number of Hindus, the largest religious minority, has been steadily decreasing since 1947 and is estimated at 10 per cent, down from 20 per cent in 1961. Hindus are concentrated in areas bordering India, such as Khulna, Jessore, Sylhet, and Dinajpur, where they constitute nearly 25 per cent of the population. The bulk of the Hindus belong to one of the lowest castes, the Namashudra, and they occupy low social and economic positions and generally follow the more inferior professions.

Smaller minorities include Buddhists, Zoroastrians (also known as Parsis,) and tribal animists. There is a Roman Catholic archbishopric at Dacca. The secular constitution guarantees the religious rights of all minorities.

In addition, there are 28 tribal groups, some of whom have been very receptive to the Christian Gospel.

**Historical Background**

Along with the rest of the Indian subcontinent, Bangladesh was part of the Indian Empire, or the British Raj. Bangladesh was one of the first territories to be subjected to the British rule; it was also one of the most restive provinces of the Empire. The British responded to frequent Bengali agitations by restricting the admission of Bengalees to the civil and military services and by partitioning Bengal in 1905.

Great Britain unwillingly acted as the engine of progress in the subcontinent, creating a political unity where there was none before. Indian nationalism was itself a product of British education that generated a body of liberal political ideas, which had no basis in either Hindu or Muslim traditions. It created the "steel framework" of Indian administration, the Indian Civil Service, which, although in modified forms, has survived virtually in tact in all the three countries that inherited the mantle of British rule.

On the negative side, British rule was responsible for the atrophy of native political and economic institutions, the exacerbation of religious rivalry between Hindus and Muslims, and the growing alienation between the Westernized and English-educated elite and the vast bulk-nearly 99 per cent of the common people deeply rooted in tradition.

The two most significant legacies of British rule in the subcontinent are generally described as the English language and the system of parliamentary democracy. Both legacies are being negated in Bangladesh. Parliamentary democracy, with such associated concepts as the rule of law, due process and freedom of speech, have been periodically suspended. The English language, as an effective medium of intercourse, may not last much longer.

**Constitution and Government**

Bangladesh is governed by the constitution of 1972 (as amended in 1973, 1974, 1975, 1977, and 1979) which established a parliamentary democracy and has not been formally suspended. This constitution incorporates four basic principles of state policy : nationalism, Islam, socialism and democracy. Under it the President is the head of state while the head of government is the Prime Minister who is responsible to the National Assembly.

Some programmes lend only to groups for group projects (Proshika), or to sub groups or individuals through their groups while holding the group responsible for repayment (BRAC, GB) or lend directly to individuals within the group. In these cases peer pressure and/or joint liability have helped in the timely repayment of loans. Group lending reduces to a certain extent the administrative cost of the lending agencies and provides an efficient way of integrating other services such as training, technical assistance, marketing and introduction to new technologies. Most of the credit funds are received from the public or private donations or subsidised credit funds. The interest rates and/or service charges are competitive and in some cases higher than the bank rates.

Viability and sustainability of the credit programmes depend on the income generated by the interest and service charges. Since these are small loans and programmes at this stage are closely supervised, the rate of interest in some cases is high enough to cover the cost. The informal credit market charges substantially higher rate of interest. Since poor women have limited access to such credit, they are eager to avail facilities offered by the specialised credit schemes. Loan recovery rate of these organisations is high due to group pressure; high level of supervision throughout the credit process; convenient repayment schedules; and better management.

Weekly repayment schedule and innovative collection procedures are important elements in the success of credit programmes for the rural poor including women, although it results in higher administrative costs for such small loans. The operating costs of these specialised credit schemes usually far exceeds the average among the National Credit Banks (NCBs) and other specialised banks. Types of income generating activities undertaken by the women, especially at the initial stage are those based on their existing skills, which ensures quick return and helps in timely loan repayment.

The soundness of the loan project and the integrity of the borrowers are more important considerations in small loans than real estate collateral. BRAC and Proshika have a system of securing 10 per cent of the amount of the proposed loan as security against bad debts. Intermediary organisations such as specialised banks, women's organisations and NGOs provide women with experience and a record of credit worthiness which women can present to formal credit institutions.

The Women's Entrepreneurial Development Programme (WEDP), Swanirvar and BRDB women's groups provide credit through formal banking system with the expectation of introducing institutional credit facilities to its members.

However, the involvement of the banks at present has been secondary. Their role has been confined to disbursing loans and managing loan accounts. It is the executing agencies or NGOs that have played the major role in organising the borrowers, preparing and recommending loan applications, supervising loan use, collecting repayments and mobilising deposits. These special credit programmes are charged initially with financing low productivity activities which will not have much effect on poverty alleviation of the borrowers. The borrowers are mostly uneducated and destitute women with minimum exposure to the outside world and with little confidence in their ability to use money to generate more money. By lending them small amount of money to undertake micro enterprises, based on their existing skills, these specialised agencies reduce the chances of failure and gradually build the confidence of such women to undertake more profitable ventures.

Studies on Grameen Bank show that the rates of return of investment in certain activities such as handloom weaving, livestock raising, shopkeeping, tailoring, sweet and *gur* making were higher than the effective rates of interest after deducting the cost of family labour, whereas rates of return were low in cases of paddy husking, mat making, cane and bamboo work.

Credit for self-employment increases the number of working days of the female borrowers who have limited employment opportunities. Study shows that 90 per cent of the female borrowers in Grameen Bank reported that since they had joined the programme, they perceived an improvement in their economic condition. Per capita income of loanee households has increased by about 32 per cent from 1980 to 1982. The primary reasons for the improvement was accumulation of capital, followed by the provision of additional employment.

A decrease in the availability of labour has been reported by the village leaders in the villages where Grameen Bank operates which has resulted in an increase in the wage rate. Daily wages for agricultural labour went up by 72 per cent from Tk. 14.2 to Tk. 24.5 between 1982 and 1985. The national annual average wage increase was 16 per cent during the same period. Grameen Bank credit has reduced dependence on local moneylenders and their high interest rate. Land being the most valuable resource in an agrarian economy, a number of women have used their income to purchase or lease lands. The per capita annual income in the target households was Tk. 3,502, which is 26 per cent higher than that of the control group. The study also shows that a significantly larger number of target households had more than one source of income. Such households also owned considerably more assets than the control groups.

The average monthly income of BRDB, MSS/MBSS members was Tk. 350 which is more than twice their income a few years ago. A study on WEDP shows that women benefited significantly since joining the programme. About 36 per cent of respondents reported gaining access to employment, while 76 per cent reported an increase in output of the products they were making and 57 per cent reported an increase in their income through the sale of their products. The quantum of increase in any of the indicators was not available from the report. An analysis of credit programmes of 13 small NGOs indicates that credit support has enabled women not only to earn extra income but also that their economic contribution has increased their status in the family thereby increasing their voice and participation in the family decision-making process.

The additional income has helped them meet the educational expenses of the children, with almost all the beneficiaries sending their school-going children to schools. Another positive impact of the credit programme is the awareness of the beneficiaries about their children's health and nutrition. Most of the special credit programmes are linked with a sustained savings mobilisation. Except WEDP, all other agencies have savings programmes for the beneficiaries. A total of Tk. 3212.2 million was generated its savings which is about three per cent of the gross national savings and five per cent of the domestic savings of the country. GB is concerned about strengthening the security base of the poor borrowers. The size of the loans and the return on the investment are too small to generate enough savings to cope with unpredictable events such as family illness, natural calamities and other emergencies. Every member of the group deposits weekly it personal savings of taka one in the Group Fund Account.

When a group member receives it loan from GB, five per cent of the loan amount is deducted its Group Tax and deposited in the Group Fund Account. The Account is managed by the group of five on a consensus basis. With the consent of the group any member can borrow from the Group Fund for both investment and consumption purposes. GB's Annual Report lists 350 different activities for which loans were granted from the Group Fund.

As of July 1994, a total of Tk. 2,398.8 million was deposited in the Group Fund by the female members and the total amount of loan disbursed from the Fund was Tk. 1,095.4 million. When a member leaves the group, she is entitled to withdraw only the personal weekly savings accumulated in the Group Fund. Individual loans vary from Tk. 200 to Tk. 1000.

The GB members also contribute a fee of five taka per thousand of loans in excess of Tk. 1000 to an Emergency Fund, basically as insurance coverage to cover default, death, disability and other accidents. The fund also offers protection against theft and loss or damage to livestock or crops. It also works as a reserve for emergency needs during major crises such its cyclone, flood or drought.

The Special Savings Fund is required when the members decide to undertake collective enterprises such as fish pond cultivation. The bank supplements the fund with a loan up to but not more than ten times the size of members' savings. Saving contribution varies between Tk. one to Tk. five per member per week. The fund is also used for other collective purposes such as construction or repair of a building for the centre, furniture or signboards.

When a member takes her second loan, she contributes Tk. one to the children's welfare fund which is used for building or making arrangements, for school rooms, for paying teachers or purchasing schoolbooks undertaking small income generating projects.

Through saving schemes, BRAC offers its members an opportunity to save their small surplus money. Group members are encouraged to make weekly savings of Tk. two in the Group Fund in order to develop savings habit and create a financial resource base to meet emergency needs and reduce their dependency on money lenders.

A Group Trust Fund is developed by deducting four per cent from all loans disbursed. As of December 1993, a total of Tk. 250.8 million had been saved by the women members. BRAC is paying six per cent interest on members' savings. Insurance policy for the members are available in BRAC. All members who have completed one year of membership in it village organisation are covered under the Life Insurance Policy. The fund is generated by a one per cent compulsory deduction from the loan disbursed.

Insurance benefits have been fixed at Tk. 5,000 and given to the nominees of the insured member on her death. Weekly savings of the members are also compulsory in Proshika-MUK and ASA. The women members in these two organisations have saved a total amount of Tk. 259 million. Women members under BRDB and RSS are also required to deposits weekly savings.

Interest on savings are paid at the existing bank rate. The Group Fund and Emergency Fund offers poor women a sense of social and economic security. Women have immediate access to their own fund as long as they work it out among themselves and they are no longer at the mercy of the local money lender.

Managing the group fund account provides the members with experience in collective management of finances. It will be an unprecedented achievement in the development field if the emergency fund/life insurance policy develops into a solid insurance plan for the poor women. There are evidences showing that women members under these special credit programmes also keep the surplus amount in their personal savings accounts, which is in general considerably higher than the group savings.

The GB is encouraging its members to keep their extra income in personal savings accounts to improve their economic strength. Women also invest their surplus income in gold, silver or corrugated iron sheet which can be liquidated in the event of an emergency or a situation requiring cash.

**Women's access financial institutions**

An assessment of the activities for which loans are disbursed indicates that women's access to formal credit has been limited. Most of the institutional credit, in the rural areas of Bangladesh is generally issued for financing agricultural inputs, fisheries, tea plantation, rural transport and small scale industries, in which women's involvement is negligible. There are three main factors which restrict women's access to institutional credit:

– Collateral requirements of the formal financial institutions,
– Lending only for traditional activities, and
– Credit procedures.

Most poor families do not have any land to offer as securities against loans. In the case of those who have land or property, land titles are generally in the name of the male "head of household".

As such, offering land as collateral means involving male members in the transaction which reduces women's control over the means of produ-ction and critical decision making. The formal financial institutions generally provide credit for agriculture and traditional non-farm activities and do not have programmes responsive to the types of work done by women.

Women entrepreneurs generally combine their business with household activities and have a combined variety of sources of sustenance. They are involved in activities like crop processing, poultry raising, horticulture and handicraft which are not in the lending portfolio of the banks. Another problem for women's access to institutional credit are formalities required by banks in sanctioning loans which are cumbersome. It is impossible for the illiterate female borrowers to fill in the complicated loan application forms. The bank personnel are also reluctant to entertain the small loan requirements of women which takes as much time as application for a large investment. The loan recovery schedules are generally not appropriate in their frequency and duration to women's needs.

Formal credit institutions are generally in the Thana centres. Bank staff seldom go to the borrowers for recovery of loans which leads to their low recovery. Total borrowing cost is also high due to hidden charges (bribe), paper and transportation costs and loss of working days in getting a loan sanctioned. Study shows that loan processing time varies between 20 days and 157 days in different financial institutions.

Special credit schemes have reached only a small portion of target women. Women need to invest in more profitable ventures which require access to increased loan amount for investment.

Most of the female borrowers are investing in small enterprises based on women's traditional occupations which generally do not generate sufficient profit margin to engage in more profitable ventures. A coordinated effort among the planners, policy makers, bankers and NGOs is needed to improve women's access to formal credit and financial institutions.

The following are the recommended measures:

- To improve women's access to formal credit and financial sector, there should be a strong advocacy programme to bring in change in the attitude of the policy makers and bankers towards women's contribution in the national economy, their credit needs and productive capacity, and their creditworthiness. They must realise that credit for self-employment is a fundamental right of women. The appropriate orientation and human qualities of bank workers at all levels is also important.
- The credit policy of the government should be reviewed thoroughly and more funds should be allocated to non-farm and other informal sector activities which absorb a large number of female labour. The policy must be formulated in such a way that female borrowers can gradually upgrade their enterprises or shift their investment from low return to high return activities.
- Women should have access to both the formal financial institutions and specialised credit schemes. The Bangladesh Bank could make separate allocations for commercial banks for credit disbursement to women which will not be transferable to male borrowers. The government, through the Bangladesh Bank, can also encourage the commercial banks to lend to women entrepreneurs through various incentive schemes such as providing preferential rediscount rate, reduced administrative fees and regulations, and deposit incentives.

– Women should be organised into groups which will provide the foundation for group guarantee of loans without any collateral. Also weekly group meetings would provide a forum for planning and implementing economic, social and community activities. Membership in a group reduces insecurity for the individuals. It also creates peer pressure for the proper utilisation of loan and its repayment on time. The size of the group should be small to be manageable.
– Educational programmes and information campaigns should be organised on a regular basis to familiarise women with the financial institutions in their area, their services, procedures and requirements.
– Loan application as well as procedures for repayment of loans should be made as simple as possible so that illiterate and semiliterate women could understand and comply with them promptly. The selection of loan activities should be left to the women borrowers, vetted by the group, who have more knowledge about women's skill and market demand for the goods. Collective savings should be encouraged which serve the dual purpose of insurance against bad debt and to meet the emergency needs of the members. The rate of interest on the loan must be market-determined to make the programme viable.
– Efforts should be made so that the bank should go to the women, not the women to the bank. Bank branches are generally located in union or thana headquarters and often in the middle of the market place. Distance as well as women's household responsibilities create problems for them to avail the services of banks. Bank workers should work with women credit and savings groups directly in the community.
– Gender desegregated data should be maintained by the banks to assess the performance of savings and credit programmes of the female clients. The policy makers and bankers should also closely monitor the bank operations to ascertain the progress and problems of financial services offered to the women clients in order to help improve future policy.

In the past, development in Bangladesh was no exception, being based mainly on agricultural production. This meant that half the population - the women - remained alienated from the mainstream of development. Polli Sree is a Bangldeshi counterpart of Community Aid Abroad that believes women must be brought into the picture if meaningful change is to be achieved. Polli Sree is a woman-headed non-government organisation that has worked in Dinajpur district, Bangladesh, for more than ten years. It now works in 117 villages, organising community groups and improving people's economic conditions, health and education.

Most of Polli Sree's programs have the aim of increasing awareness about gender issues, as well as empowering poor women and girls by increasing their knowledge and skills, and giving them greater access to financial support. One of the main strategies for empowering poor women has been the formation of women's groups. These are brought together by field workers to discuss common problems and accumulate resources through weekly savings plans. To begin with, field workers may visit poor women to discuss issues, then bring women together to support one another. In three years, 354 women's groups and 29 men's groups were formed, involving almost 7,000 poor Bangladeshis. One woman member described the difference being in a women's group has made to her life, "We can now discuss our own problems in a group and decide on what to do. When we were married, marriages were not registered, but now we don't let anybody's marriage go unregistered."

According to group members, the program has also had a real effect on the prevalence of practices like dowry, polygamy, child marriage, trafficking in women and children and the difficulties caused by money-lenders. The savings aspect of group activities has also had a real effect on women's lives: "Our power in the family has increased familial issues are discussed now with us and decisions are taken jointly. Decisions on family expenses are also taken jointly." Another aspect of Polli Sree's work has been an adult literacy program. This program is targeted at those who didn't get an opportunity for formal schooling, particularly underprivileged rural women. In three years, well over a thousand people -

most of them women - enrolled in the course.

According to an evaluation, for Polli Sree, the rate of learning by program participants who had almost no previous literacy or numeracy skills was "quite astonishing". After the program, participants reported now being able to read and understand contract documents (such as for labour) they were required to sign, as well as signs and posters, increasing their knowledge about many things.

A very important flow-on effect of the literacy program has been the adult learners' increased awareness of the importance of education; enrolments of their children in primary school have gone up, and many of the adult learners expressed a hope that the Polli Sree program would in future focus on children who have had to drop out of formal schooling. Overall, Polli Sree's range of programs have had positive effects on the lives of women and girls in Bangladesh in many ways.

One of the most concrete examples of a change in attitudes toward gender was a colourful rally organised for Women's Day, with banners depicting different gender issues. Some future directions for the program include the expansion of the credit program for funding income-generating projects, and making gender-awareness programs available to boys as well as girls, so that everyone can be involved in this kind of social change.

Many of Community Aid Abroad's programs around the world have a focus on gender; on trying to ensure that both women and men benefit from development. At a basic level, this means ensuring women have access to programs such as literacy classes, agricultural training or micro-credit schemes; yet perhaps the most important effect of many such programs is that they provide a space for women to work together for changes in many other areas of their lives.

The Barendra Development Organisation is a partner of Community Aid Abroad, working in Naogaon District, a very poor area in north-west Bangladesh. Naogaon District's social and economic infrastructure is very limited: the area has little irrigation for farming, poor roads and under-resourced schools and health facilities. This lack of social infrastructure—coupled with a very conservative local community—means that discrimination against women is an entrenched part of everyday life in the area. Barendra Development Organisation (BDO), a local Bangladeshi non-government organisation, tackles this discrimination head on.

BDO takes the approach that dealing with women's economic issues and their access to resources is not enough to really change women's lives; in general they also need greater power over decision-making in their families and communities. To achieve this, BDO works with local women's groups, such as the Tularbayal Landless Women Society. For many years, the women of Tularbayal village have lived in "purdah"; their movements very restricted in public. According to BDO, in very poor areas like Tularbayal, purdah not only disempowers women, but means that their families can literally starve, because women are not able to work outside the home.

BDO used literacy programs as a way of raising issues with women like those in Tularbayal. In these classes, women not only learn basic literacy and numeracy, but have the opportunity to discuss social relations in their community, their rights, and how the law and government works. This has proved to be an empowering process for many of the women, enabling them to work together for change in their communities.

Chen Banu, head of the Tularbayal Landless Women Society, gave examples of how the group now take on social issues in their community and families. They have pushed for access to land and resources in their community, and are now able to use thirty village ponds to grow fish for sale. They have also begun a class action against a local landlord over land issues. The group has identified a number of other important social issues, including dowry, domestic violence, and child marriage. Chen Banu explains that they have two approaches to these issues.

The first is to raise the awareness of both men and women; their rights and responsibilities, and the relevant laws. To begin with the group held workshops for women on the issues, but when men in the community took issue with the workshops, they became open to both women and men. Their second approach is to directly confront the issue when it affects group members. For example, if a member of the group experiences domestic violence, the other members of the group directly confront the man, and try to convince him to stop. This solidarity between women in groups like the Tularbayal Landless Women Society is one of the most important factors in enabling women to make real changes in their own lives.

# 2

# Education and Employment

## Education and Identity

Many of Community Aid Abroad's programs around the world involve basic education in some form. Our broad education philosophy involves developing the knowledge, skills and confidence of communities, to enable them to advocate for their own rights. Article 15 of the Draft Declaration of the Rights of Indigenous Peoples states: "Indigenous children have the right to all levels and forms of education of the state. All Indigenous Peoples also have this right and the right to establish and control their educational systems and institutions providing education in their own languages, in a manner appropriate to their cultural methods of teaching and learning." Education is a basic human right and the responsibility of government to provide, yet formal education - when available - often fails to meet people's needs. Indigenous peoples in particular often find that mainstream education systems are alienating and do not value their own culture or language. Here Lia Kent, Mark Deasey, Patrick Kilby and Justin Coburn from Community Aid Abroad's program section explain some of the ways in which our programs can work to increase people's access to appropriate education.

## Awareness-raising and Literacy in Bangladesh

The Barendara Development Organisation (BDO) is a long-standing partner of Community Aid Abroad in Bangladesh. They work in impoverished north-west Bangladesh, where women have lived in traditional "purdah" - or effective social isolation - until very recently. The change came with the work of BDO in the area of adult literacy for women: for a couple of hours every week for six months, students are taught the literacy and numeracy through the discussion of social issues such as women's rights.

The women of the Tulanbayal Landless Women's Society in Paroil Village, north-west Bangladesh, said that the training made them more aware of the principle of equal rights for men and women, and of their rights within the family. Other students said the training made them more aware of the importance of education for their children, and gave them greater self-awareness and confidence to make changes in their families, in their villages, and more broadly in their dealings with government. As a result the women had begun addressing issues of domestic violence by the husbands of group members, lobbying local government to make available land for the landless group members, and lobbying for the release of a community pond for their use to farm fish.

**Women who win Bangladesh**

The gold nose ring was precious to Hoosenera, a woman from a village in Bangladesh. But she had no choice. She either sold the gold ring for cash, or she could not help her 13-year old son to get a job in a carpet factory. Hoosenera had already given her 15-year old daughter away in marriage to a relative. Desperate for cash, she sold her gold nose ring. Her story of struggle is typical of so many women in rural Bangladesh. No choices. And no opportunities to make informed decisions about her life there seemed to be no escape from poverty. Today, your aware donations are providing real choices and long-term opportunities for women like Hoosenera. Hoosenera lives with her five children in a village in the District of Dinajpur in Bangladesh. Her husband left her and the children four years ago. Hoosenera now works as a domestic helper to a school teacher in her village. Her income? Just half a kilo of rice and two meals a day.

**Sun Flower**

Hoosenera heard about a group which helps desolate women. It's run by a community group called Sun Flower. This non-government group works with support that includes your Community Aid Abroad aware donations.. Rather than bring in outside experts, Community Aid Abroad works with local project partners like Sun Flower to overcome poverty and work for social justice.

Sun Flower is developing 90 community groups in 26 villages. People benefit from savings and loans with the credit union, literacy classes, and pre-school centres. Mother and child health care centres are being organised and promoted. Some 1000 members will be provided with awareness-raising training and 200 will receive leadership training. Hoosenera joined a group of women meeting each week. They were encouraged to save and participate in a 'revolving loan' scheme. This scheme involves people borrowing money to establish a small business.

**Open doors**

Women like Hoosenera also joined functional literacy classes. Learning to read and write for day to day living is a major step towards breaking out of poverty. For example, people can read money-lending contracts, medicine labels or local government messages that have an impact on their lives. Six months after joining the group, Hoosenera was entitled to a loan of 1500 TK. This opened the door to a regular weekly income. Hoosenera paid for paddy (raw rice) which she husked and sold. She saved enough cash to buy a rickshaw for 2400 TK (about A$92). She rented the rickshaw to a friend of her brother. Membership of the group opened other doors: training sessions on nutrition, mother and child care, water and sanitation, family planning and other health issues. The group also trains Traditional Birth Attendants to reduce infant mortality. Hoosenera's daughter lost her first baby through lack of medical help. When her daughter was having her second baby, Hoosenera invited her to stay - she had become aware how much the child care and health program had improved conditions in her village. Hoosenera she said her life had been completely changed for the better. She was literate, financially independent and aware of her children's need for education, including her youngest daughter. Like Hoosenera, this woman gains an income husking raw rice.

**Choices**

Hoosenera now joins in campaigns on child marriage and registering marriages. She proudly says that the days of 'thumb impressions' to mark her name are gone. And she told me that the person who hires her rickshaw has shown interest in getting married to her! That's a decision she says she needs to be made carefully. Hoosenera is now able to make choices, to make informed decisions. No longer does she need someone to support her. She no longer feels she is a commodity.

**Women Gain From Group Formation**

Poverty is widespread in Bangladesh, especially in the north-west of the country where Community Aid Abroad focuses its program. Landlessness, exploitation of tribal communities, lack of income and opportunities are particular problems for the thousands of people living in remote rural villages. The poorest of the poor are often women who do not have the income earning potential of men but who carry a heavy domestic workload and suffer from second class social status. In assisting village people to tackle these problems the Community Aid Abroad field office in Bangladesh identifies and assesses local community organisations who work directly with the poor, ultimately assisting them to form their own people's organisations.

To partly address this situation Community Aid Abroad funded several years ago a well known group and long standing Community Aid Abroad partner in Dinajpur District, Shahid Srimity Sangha, to provide training and encouragement to small voluntary groups who were motivated to work in the villages. One of the success stories of this program is Gram Bikash Kendra (GBK) and its women's literacy, awareness raising and savings and loan project.

GBK was formed in 1988 by a group of concerned people with the aim of building and strengthening organisation of the rural poor, especially women, to develop the capacity and to improve their own situation through self-help and collective action. Over a four year period GBK conducted surveys in the villages, had lengthy discussions with village people, raised awareness and formed voluntary community groups. They also built their own capacity, benefiting from the training provided by Shahid Srimity Sangha and in 1992 they became a registered community organisation with the Bangladesh Government and began to receive direct Community Aid Abroad funding and support for their program.

Through extensive community consultations GBK has now assisted the formation of 46 village groups throughout the district with a total membership of 800 people. Most of the members are women as women have been specifically targeted as the poorest and most oppressed in the community. Usually these consultations would take several months before a group is formed and concentrate on helping women to identify the causes of their poverty and possible joint action and self help projects. A recent visit to GBK-supported villages showed the significant changes which can take place in women's lives through the process of community development. One women commented that "GBK has helped us to see things we couldn't see". With greater awareness of the possibilities of joint action the women have formed a functional literacy class led by a GBK field worker and now have a basic understanding of literacy and numeracy. As well as enhancing women's confidence and solidarity there are practical benefits such as the ability to sign for wages received after a day's labour in the fields with the knowledge that the correct amount was being paid, rather than ignorantly placing a thumbprint in the wages book. Women who would previously have hidden in their houses now had the confidence to speak publicly to outsiders and were generally vocal and articulate. The mutual support offered by the group had enabled the women to successfully demand medicines from a government clinic and to intervene in a case of domestic violence. It is important that women are able to gain economically from participation in a group as this will lead eventually to an increase in standards of living. Consequently, GBK places emphasis on a small scale savings and loan program through which women can save small amounts per week from selling eggs or rice or from daily labour in the planting and harvest seasons. One member is trained to operate a bank account and the savings are pooled. When cash is needed for a medical emergency, festival, etc. a woman can draw on her savings or take a loan from the joint account rather than borrow money at extortionate interest rates from moneylenders. As the poor often need to borrow money to make ends meet there is a significant saving in interest. Once the savings scheme is well established loans can be made for income generating activities. In one village a group of 17 women had saved Taka 4000 ($160) over a two year period and are making loans to members for duck rearing which generates income from the sale of eggs and the sale of ducks gained from natural increase.

GBK will receive continuing assistance from Community Aid Abroad to support and expand the women's groups. GBK participates in a network of Community Aid Abroad partners in north-west Bangladesh which concentrates on training and mutual support. Community Aid Abroad funds for this project will cover the cost of salaries for GBK field workers and literacy teachers, functional literacy materials and lamps and fuel so that classes can be conducted in the evenings. Most importantly, contribution will continue the process of community development and enhanced dignity for women in north-west Bangladesh.

**Education is the key**

Two things struck me about Bangladesh. One, the obvious, water everywhere; canals, ponds, lakes, rivers, flooded paddy fields, puddles. The other, a remarkable absence of women in towns and villages. Unlike India or Sri Lanka, where women move freely and take very public roles, in rural Bangladesh they seem hidden away, reflecting their low status and disadvantage. To reach our women's project, it was not surprising to have to get there by small boat. We paddled down the clear, fast moving river that forms the border with India, on either side border-post towns nestling in the trees. Upon landing we joined a class on a small mud verandah with twenty women of all ages sitting cross-legged. The teacher was a young, trained woman from the village who stood confidently before her peers and taught them their alphabet script.

**Functional Literacy**

As the teacher wrote words on the board, the women got up one by one to overwrite and copy the letters until they got them right. The words they learn have daily relevance - four new words a lesson. This painstaking learning unlocks basic documents, signposts, newspapers and, for some, the price of things they need to buy.

This is functional literacy in Bangladesh, in a village near

Dijnapur in the Northwest. The women are there because they want to be there - even though it means that never-ending household tasks will pile up. It is clearly easier for younger women; still, the odd granny sits amongst them. Most of these women have lost their assets, often through indebtedness. They are so poor that when disaster strikes - it often does in Bangladesh - they must sell everything they have to feed themselves. Being illiterate and uneducated, as most are, means that they have no idea of their rights and become vulnerable to extortionate money lenders.

To see adult women grappling with literacy and numeracy for the first time makes you realise what a deprivation lack of education is. Effectively these women have been shut out of a level of communication just as important as sight or hearing. For most, the results have been immensely negative. But until you learn the power of reading you cannot fully comprehend what you've missed. The transformation from downtrodden, apathetic victims to motivated, energetic, independent women is quite extraordinary. It is as if they have had a veil of oppression lifted from their eyes. Through the functional literacy class, they begin to discuss bigger questions: why are they poor, what sort of relations should exist between men and women, and what future do they see for their daughters. Whilst not rejecting the broad role of women in this traditional muslim society, these women want their daughters to be educated, to have some financial independence and greater choice, especially over matters like how many children they will have. The project, run by a women's organisation called Polli Sree (meaning Rural Beauty), forges a fundamental psychological change towards optimism and self belief.

Perhaps the most striking aspect is how forward-looking these women are, and how excited they are at the prospect of planning a future - not being subject merely to fate. Polli Sree is led by a charismatic woman, Shamima Ara Begun, in a country where most organisations are run by men. Community Aid Abroad's funding is quite small, but targeted. The non-funding relationship is just as important - our Field Officer, Julu, provides support in the form of advice, mentoring and connecting Polli Sree with other like-minded organisations. Education is a fundamental keystone for any effective development with poor people and a vital basic human right. This issue of HoriZons is about the 10 basic human rights to coincide with the launch of the Community Aid Abroad Rights Campaign. Together we can end poverty and injustice by getting basic human rights fully recognised for all.

Bangladesh as one of the most high density countries in the world face many problems of poverty, such as high illiteracy rate and low access to health care. The situation of the country has improved concerning food supply, immunisation of children and access to safe drinking water. Life expectancy has also risen. Bangladesh is also known as a country of NGOs. It has a large part community development organisations, most of the NGOs are small but growing fast. Some of the organisations have been successful in organising the rural poor and eradicating poverty. The NGOs in Bangladesh began their work as village co-operative systems. Even though the developing of the communities motivation, education and training was important, the work did not alone change the greater structural problems of the society. The focus is now on the grassroots level. Focusing on who is ensuring services to local poor and complementing the rural public sectors, which often have failed in reaching the poor. Thus, the local organisations and NGOs have emerged with a new generation of ideas to fight against poverty and gender inequality. Donors have also played their role in initiating the process. A significant feature of this phenomenon of grassroots NGOs has been the rise of organisations providing a fora for the unorganised poor rural women. Various kinds of women's organisations work in Bangladesh. The traditional women's organisations has been focusing on delivering such as women's education and health service. However, this approach has been inadequate to address the strategic needs of the women.

**Role of NGOs and Empowerment**

NGOs in Bangladesh do not only see women's economic empowerment as its goal, but encourages uniting of the poor women in groups as part of a larger struggle. If the programmes are undertaken collectively they are more likely to achieve their goals than otherwise. Credit based income generating activities are the main tasks for most of the NGOs.

Credit programmes can be a means to women's empowerment. Credit programmes begin by organising poor rural women into small groups. The group formation among the women helps generating peer group support and solidarity. Through meetings the awareness process starts. After selecting a specific income generating project they are given training.

The concept of time and regularity becomes important as a strict discipline with weekly savings are established. Issue-based meetings is a forum where each credit group member must participate, they chose issues which are important to their lives such as immunisation of children, family planning, school issues, legal issues etc. Through the credit group the women have access to money. The money borrowed from the NGO helps them raise their position towards their husband and other house hold members, and their self-confidence is increased. As a result their practical needs are largely fulfilled and their strategic needs are recognised by the family and the community, as both their conditions and positions begin to change. The credit programmes have a visible impact on the women's empowerment. The women's bargaining position in the home increases as they enhance their economic contribution to the family. The strength of earning an income together with the strength of belonging to a group help women establish new roles for themselves. However, there may also be threats, such as if the women hand over the money to their husbands they may be more dependent of the husbands, and gender inequality will be reinforced. The non-economic support also help organising the group formation for the credit program. The governmental formal education often helps to reinforce the women's domestic role and does not bring about any change in social relations either within or outside the family. The non-formal education run by the NGOs on the other hand seeks to promote consciousness among the women about gender inequality so that women not only understand the causes of their oppression but also take steps to improve their conditions.

**Constraints Encountered**

Multi-dimensional difficulties and constraints have been encountered in the work for women's empowerment. Most of the violence towards women in Bangladesh take place within the households. The reported cases of violence are increasing. There are two reasons for this. First of all the increased awareness of violence against women has facilitated uncovering occurrence of violence. Secondly, rural women are at a crossroad now and have been faced with the ideology of patriarchy which help reinforce the power hierarchies within the family.

The increasing trend of violence against women should therefore be explained as the outcome of a contradiction against the ideology of patriarchy, manifested in social restrictions against women's mobility, the system of early marriage for girls, restriction on negotiation rights etc. A classic case of patriarchy is the assumption that the male must exercise control over women by limiting her mobility to the home. Such control of female sexuality is further elevated by creating an image of the mother as divine and women who do not live up to the ideal, as "fallen women". In Bangladesh the family is the breading grounds for some of the most persistent discrimination against women, such as sexual subordination of women, restriction of the mobility of women and different access to resources within the family.

The NGOs are still facing difficulties when trying to convince the women that gender inequalities are not natural but a social construction.

**Empowerment and Reproductive Health**

The issue of contraceptive use is well researched in Bangladesh. It has been found that the engagement of women in credit group activities and empowerment are positively linked with the use of contraceptives. The success of increasing the use of contraceptives in Bangladesh in spite of the lack of economic development was made possible through the massive door-to-door supply service that has been provided throughout the country. This programme may itself have had a consciousness raising effect on the rural population.

When the contraceptive knowledge is universal and the social costs to use contraceptives has been reduced it has led to a rise in use of contraceptive. If the development programmes tackle the sources of subordination, provide access to information, help women to gain self esteem and ability to control their own affairs, they will increase the possibilities of creating a context in which use of contraceptives will rise. The credit empowerment process addresses the structural problems as the power relations change and the women's bargaining situation improves. The social context of the rural women has been changing as the economic life has become more complex. The women engaged in self-help projects and credit groups have managed better in the new situation. Many of them have accepted that the use of contraception can be economically beneficial as fewer children are born. Women's growing sense of self respect and bargaining capacity within the household may have diminished the men's resistance towards contraceptives. Women's reproductive rights and empowerment goes together. Increasing the status of women also enhance their decision-making capacity, especially concerning sexuality and reproduction. This is essential for the long-term success of the population programmes. It is also important to increase access to health service to succeed with the programmes. Both these facts have now been recognised by government. Even though most of the NGOs in Bangladesh do not directly provide health services they contribute greatly through promoting the messages that women should have control over their own body and the right to decide over when and how many children they should have. The participation in such programmes by poor women may lead to a dynamic process social development with increased empowerment and self confidence.

**Social Development**

Poverty and under development were assumed to put all members of affected households - men, women, and children - at an equal disadvantage. "Households" were regarded as static entities where labor and resources are pooled and equally shared. The implicit conclusion was that changes thought of as beneficial for development would be neutral in their effects on the different members of the households. Empirical evidence revealed, however, that the costs and benefits of development are often disproportionately distributed, depending on an individual member's sex, age, and relationship to the household head.

Particularly in traditional societies with a pronounced gender-specific division of labor, which accords women and their work lower status or social importance, it cannot be assumed that females will automatically benefit from an increase in the "household" income. At best, the provision of goods, for which men are traditionally responsible, improves. Experience shows that getting through to women means that children are also reached. Although today there is a wider recognition of the importance of women in the process of development, the prevailing nature of interventions toward them is welfare-oriented rather than income-generating. Social welfare projects or "female"" components in projects (for example, maternal and child health, family planning, hygiene, nutrition, home economics, and kitchen gardening) focus mainly on the domestic role of women as homemakers and childrearers, succumbing to the fiction of a constant "household" with a male breadwinner. Such interventions, as important as they are, meet with little success in getting women out of poverty, nor do they alter the fundamental problem of women's dependence on conjugal ties for access to resources. Income-generating projects, in contrast, try to create a situation that helps women support themselves and their families without welfare.

They involve upgrading existing skills or teaching new ones, providing the resources needed to use the skills in the production of marketable goods and services, providing marketing assistance, promoting wage employment, raising awareness of the root causes of poverty, teaching functional and legal literacy, and encouraging women to participate in community-level decision-making. Of course, the "status of women" as well as the factors that confer status vary considerably across regions. A woman's status is often described in terms of her income, employment, education, health, and fertility, as well as the roles she plays within the family, the community and society. It also involves society's perception of these roles and the value it places on them. The status of women implies a comparison with the status of men, and is therefore a significant reflection of the level of social justice in a society.

UNDP's Human Development Report 1995 reveals how things look for women in this respect: "Men generally fare better than women on almost every socio-economic indicator (except life expectancy since, for biological reasons, women tend to live longer than men)." Gender disparities exist in every country. While in industrial countries women get less than two-thirds of the employment opportunities and about half the earnings of men, gender-discrimination in developing countries is much more broadly based. It occurs not only in employment but also in education, nutritional support and health care. Illiteracy is always higher for women-who make up two-thirds of the illiterate population. And neglect of women's health and nutrition is so serious in some countries, particularly in Asia, that it even outweighs women's natural biological tendency to live longer than men. Considering these early deaths, as well as those from the infanticide of girl-babies, some studies estimate that up to 100 million women are "missing."

**Poverty in Bangladesh**

Located in one of the world's most disaster-prone natural environments, Bangladesh exhibits one of the worst profiles of human deprivation.

**Profile of Human Deprivation in Bangladesh**

| | |
|---|---|
| Population (mid-1995) | 119.3 million |
| People in absolute poverty total (1992) | 93.2 million (78%) |
| rural (1992) | 84.3 million (71%) |
| Population without access to: | |
| health services (1985-93) | 62.0 million (52%) |
| safe water (1988-93) | 18.0 million (15%) |
| sanitation (1988-93) | 77.8 million (65%) |
| Population growth rate (1995) | 2.4 |
| Life expectancy at birth (1995) | 55 years |
| Adult literacy rate (1992) | 36.4% |
| Enrolment ratio for all levels (percentage 6-23) (1992) | 32% |
| Low birthweight babies (1991) | 34% |
| Infant mortality rate per 1,000 live births (1995) | 108 |
| Underweight children | 66% |
| Under-5 mortality rate per 1,000 live births (1993) | 164 |

This general picture of misery, however, obscures the inequalities in the distribution human deprivation among subgroups of the poor, in particular among men and women.

Poverty and underdevelopment, rapidly growing numbers of people are finding themselves without enough land to satisfy their basic needs and without any substantial hope of gainful employment. This fundamental problem of landlessness and unemployment is in large part caused and perpetuated by high population growth, low educational levels and socio-economic power structures resulting in the concentration of productive lands in the hands of a relatively small number of wealthy households.

**Female-Male Gaps in Bangladesh**

| *Indicators* | *Females as a percentage of males** |
|---|---|
| Life expectancy (1992) | 99-100 |
| Population (1992) | 94 |
| Adult female literacy (1992) | 51 |
| Years of schooling (1992) | 29 |
| Enrolment rates (1990) | |
| primary | 86 |
| secondary | 50 |
| tertiary | 27 |
| Economically active women (1994) | 73 |

As a consequence, the poorest are forced in growing numbers to settle on lands that are particularly affected by the yearly recurring natural disasters like floods and cyclones, claiming many lives and leaving innumerable destitutes, especially women and children. But there are creeping disasters as well which have more dreadful implications on the environment, the population, and the economy than the sudden ones: riverine erosion and drought. In a situation of increasing landlessness, high rates of unemployment, natural disaster threats, especially embankment people as well as the floating people have been compelled to live with poverty, hunger, disease, illiteracy, and homelessness. Human misery everywhere in the country is, however, most acutely felt by women, because they additionally face cultural forces which severely impact on every sphere of their lives.

## Women's Health and Nutritional Security in Bangladesh

Where socio-economic conditions are poor, the health of

the whole community is threatened. Where gender biases favour males, however, women and female children are particularly vulnerable to health risks. Simply treating a woman's state of health as a biomedical problem is thus not enough. Apart from economic and environmental conditions, a woman's health is profoundly influenced by social customs and cultural traditions.

Many of the health problems that affect women have their roots in childhood. Due to son preference, girls suffer not only nutritional neglect, they also receive less attention during sickness than boys. According to the 1995 Human Development Report, 59% of girls suffer chronic malnutrition, whereas the figure for boys is 56%. The number of girls who die before the age of five exceeds that of boys by 11% - which may be interpreted as preferential access to health care.

Preferential food allocation to males exacerbates malnutrition among females, who eat last and least throughout their lives. Even in their reproductive years, women appear to receive less from the family pot than men, irrespective of economic class: 77% of pregnant women from middle-income households and more than 95% of those from low income households weigh less than the standard of 50 kilograms. The prevalence of infection and parasitic diseases in poor communities compounds the problem.

The high maternal mortality rate of 600 deaths per 100,000 live births is the tragic evidence that also women's specific health needs suffer considerable neglect: 58% of the pregnant women aged fifteen to forty-nine suffer from anaemia, and only 5% of births are attended by trained health personnel according to UNDP. Moreover, those women, who are already in poorest physical shape, rarely get the rest they need, particularly during pregnancy. A UNDP time-use study reveals that in Bangladesh a woman's work burden is 10% higher than men's. It is very unlikely, especially under conditions of permanent struggles to survive and frequent childbearing, that women can reduce their working time during pregnancy. According to a World Bank Country Study, the main reasons for the high maternal mortality rate are young age and frequent pregnancies as well as the women's precarious state of nutrition - a lifetime of inadequate food intake results in insufficient growth and pelvic development for childbearing. Between 16% and 25% of the maternal deaths are attributed to abortions under unhygienic conditions. Another 20% succumb to eclampsia (a convulsive condition during pregnancy resulting in coma and death). A further 5-10% die of postpartum sepsis and the same number of tetanus. The remaining major causes are bleeding, prolonged labor, and violent deaths.

Especially in times of acute underemployment and economic distress, family conflicts often degenerate into violent acts against women. A study carried out over a period of about ten years documents that rape, physical torture and murder of woman are nothing unusual in times of crisis, and that it is precisely women from the lower classes who frequently suffer from anxiety neuroses and depressions. In a society where the perceived honour of the family hinges on the virtue of its female members, rape has especially tragic social consequences for the victim: the shame falls not on the ravisher but upon the ravished.

**Education**

The average educational level of women in Bangladesh is lower than that of men, which is itself shaky enough in comparison with other poor countries. The same applies to primary schooling. In number of school years completed, females lag far behind males especially in rural areas. Many factors have an influence on women's educational opportunities. Most studies point to poverty as the principal reason why families either fail to enrol their girls in school or withdraw them prematurely from primary school. It is not just that the direct and indirect costs of school attendance are beyond their means, but also that the children are needed at home to perform duties that fall preponderantly on the girls. Extra income plays only a secondary role in the widespread labor demand for girls, since most of them have to work as unpaid labor: in 1990, 3.4% of the girls in the age group ten to fourteen were reported as "economically active".

Prevailing cultural values and norms appear to have far more significance in the low state of female education, however. Many parents in rural areas lack interest or are openly hostile to the formal education of their daughters for reasons related to social and religious norms in general and to marriage prospects in particular. The opinion is still quite widespread that education spoils a girl's character and undermines her willingness to fulfil her traditional role. Early marriage and the importance of preserving a girl's good reputation lead to widespread withdrawal of girls from school at puberty, especially if they attend coeducational institutions.

**Marriage**

Early marriage, which is a reflection of the low status of women and their low educational attainment, is also a social custom favoring high fertility as well as high maternal mortality. The average age at which girls marry has slightly gone up, though, from 16.4 years in 1970 to 18 years in 1990. According to the Muslim code of religious law, girls should be wedded at puberty, which can have its onset quite early. An unmarried daughter who is beyond puberty often is still felt to be an embarrassment to the family. Since their economic value is perceived as low, girls are considered a burden on the parental home. Yet at the same time strict norms of behaviour keep them from taking up income earning work. As a rule, the marriage is arranged by the father or another male guardian. Bride and bridegroom do have the right to turn down a match, but it is not customary to make use of this right. Most girls are married to men who are considerably older than themselves. The age difference - averaging seven years at present - confers an additional aura of marital authority on the husbands. The Dowry Prohibition Act of 1989 forbids the giving and accepting of a dowry under penalty of fine or even prison, but this traditional practice continues nevertheless. If the dowry does not correspond to what the bridegroom or his parents demand, the marriage pact can be broken off, in which case the family of the bride is socially disgraced. As protection against utter destitution should she lose her husband through separation or death, under Islamic law a Bangladeshi woman can lay claim on a certain sum from him, the Mohorana, to be given her either when she marries or in case of divorce.

But this does not happen either; first, because many women are not aware of this right and second, because insisting on it would expose a woman to social censure and the risk of losing her husband's goodwill. If a woman does demand the Mohorana in case of divorce, then her chances of remarrying plummet. In her husband's family, the wife is subordinate to all the other members of the household - females included. Her only path to social recognition is through motherhood. Male progeny are preferred because, among other reasons, they inherit and it is their duty to provide for the elderly. Owing to the age difference among married couples, women run a high risk of being widowed, with the consequent danger of being left impoverished. In most cases they move out of their parental home without any kind of material cushion that would lend them security and independence. Since under Muslim law women are only inconsequentially entitled to inherit, they must depend on their sons to look after them. This fundamental dependency provides a strong incentive to women to bear as many children as possible and as early as possible as a risk insurance against abrupt poverty.

Over and above the constitution in Bangladesh stands the patriarchal interpretation of the law and the religion, which makes implementing egalitarian legislation extremely problematic. Under the constitution, both sexes have the same rights and are entitled to equal treatment under the law. Women also have the right to vote. But a low educational level, illiteracy, a feeble social and political awareness, and the duty to adhere to religious and cultural norms, all act to keep women from taking part in public life. In family matters such as marriage, divorce, guardianship for children, and rights of inheritance, most people are guided by religious laws, which discriminate quite clearly against women.

Under the Islamic law of inheritance, widows receive but a trifling portion of their husband's estate, most particularly if there are no children or "only" daughters. In the absence of a son as male heir, most of the estate passes to the male relatives of the deceased. This law gives women another strong motivation to bear many children. As a rule the wife waives the right to the share (minuscule in any case) due her by law from her husband or parents so as not to jeopardize her chances of assistance in case of acute emergency.

Discrimination against women is further evidenced by the unilateral laws governing polygamy and divorce. Whereas a man can reject his wife without a civil divorce, a woman must go through long drawn-out court proceedings. The guardianship over children belongs to the husband or to an older male family member. The mother has the duty to care for the sons until they are seven years old, the daughters until puberty. This she is not permitted to do, however, if she marries a second time or, in the judgement of religious doctrine, leads an "immoral" life, i.e. fails to conform to the strictures of Purdah.

**Purdah**

The overwhelming majority of women in rural Bangladesh, not only live in grinding poverty but are also women is encoded in *Purdah - the moral obligation of the woman to live in seclusion, in submission and with modesty.*

In Bangladesh Purdah is manifested as the strict limitation of women's mobility outside their homestead (bari). Women who leave their homestead and enter the public male domain must dress so that body and face are covered. Not to do so would be held a provocative and public offence and would blemish the family's repute. The segregation of the sexes makes the labor market virtually off limits to women. In 1993, the female share of the labor force was a mere 8%. Observance of Purdah earns high social and religious prestige, but only the more affluent can afford to stick strictly to the rules. Men work primarily as agricultural laborers or producers; they are likewise responsible for the selling of agricultural produce and for purchases on the markets. Women, in contrast, are restricted to activities that can be performed within their homestead, as for example, the preparation of foods that are sold in the village or at urban markets as finished products, small livestock keeping, and handicrafts such as spinning, weaving, or needlework. The advantage of such extremely low-paid at-home work is that it collides least with a woman's duties as housewife and mother and with the prescriptions of purdah. The isolation of the woman thus kept busy puts the seal on her powerlessness and ensures male dominance. For »reasons of respectability« women are not allowed to trade in public. Normally it is the men who bring the product to market and transact business. Often, however, it is also prepubescent girls or post menopausal women, who do not yet or no longer pose a «danger» to society. With poverty on the increase, however, women are being forced more and more to venture into male domains.

The gradual opening of the labor market for them is a two-edged sword, however. Purdah remains so powerful a normative code of proper conduct that manual labor in public brings women appreciable loss of status, exposing them to psychic stress and insecurity. The reputability of the whole family hinges on the «invisibility» of the woman. Her visible presence in road construction and similar work sectors is a sign of great poverty and desperation - otherwise women would not take on such jobs. The other side of the coin is the opportunity for social change resulting from the emergence of women from their traditional condition of dependence. The reason for the growing popularity of female labor is not difficult to guess: under the pretence that their weaker physical constitution makes them much less productive they are as a rule paid notably less than men.

**Women's Entitlements in Rural Bangladesh**

Under the rigid rules defining the place and role of the sexes in rural Bangladesh, women are fettered by the contradictions of their purdah-dictated status, which sharply curtails their entitlement to productive resources and even their own labor, while the men's obligation to protect and support the women is governed by normative control. So whereas women's traditional duties continue to be valid unchanged, their normative entitlements are being worn away by advancing relativism, a process that spreading poverty makes particularly acute. It is no surprise that in a social environment such as this, women have scant chance of surviving in a way befitting human dignity.

The relative validity of normative entitlements means that, with respect to nutrition and health, the intra-household allocation of resources by no means corresponds to the members' needs. Rather it is determined by the individual's place in the family hierarchy, which depends in turn on age, sex and relationship to the household head. This traditional asymmetry in satisfying basic needs translates under condition of absolute poverty into a higher incidence of illness and mortality among women and girls. Women's institutionally limited access to resources and their excessively high dependence on normatively codified entitlements produce specifically gender-linked differences in the process of impoverishment. In 1979 Mead Cain depicted an example of what happens - an example more pertinent than ever today to the lot of rural women: "One of the women in our sample was the second wife of a relatively rich man. She had been married previously and had a number of children by her former husband. By the time she married for the second time, two of her children had died and one daughter was already married. Her only living son joined her in her new husband's household. The rich husband also had children by his first wife, all of whom had grown up and established their own households by the time of his second marriage. When, several years after the second marriage, the man died, all his land passed to the children of his first wife. Because the second wife bore him no children, neither she nor her son had any claim to his property upon his death. For various reasons, the widow was unable to turn to the family of her first husband for help. Consequently, she was left with no means of support for herself or her son. She survived by begging, travelling daily to Mymensingh Town (over eight kilometers away) for this purpose.

She was permitted to maintain a hut in her deceased husbands' bari, and she continues to live there with her son. Next to her hut lives one of her stepsons and his family who, aside from occasional handouts, offer her no support. Ironically, the bari of her deceased second husband is perhaps the richest per capita in the village, and her brother-in-law, who lives in the same bari, is by far the richest man in the village. None of this, however has done the widow any good." The story shows how dependent the economic status is on that of their husband's and how abruptly they can be plunged into destitution. Because of the striking age differences among married couples, early widowhood before the sons of a union reach employable age is a widespread occurrence.

The increasing number of households headed by women is a further indication of how normative entitlements are eroding. More and more men from the poor strata no longer earn enough to provide for their families. Many leave home for a time or even for good to seek work in the cities. "Seasonal" divorces are the result, particularly in periods of acute food scarcity. For women, then, the impoverishment process proceeds along several tracks. They become poorer along with the rest of the family, and through the breakdown of the household and the attendant loss of their normative entitlements.

**Changing Faces of Women in Bangladesh**

Muslim women live in Jiala, a small village in the Satkhira district of southwest Bangladesh, near the Indian border. They are rarely addressed by their given names. They are wives (bou) and mothers (ma), brother's wives (chachee or mamee) or mothers-in-law (shashoree). While they are also farmers, rice sellers, milk venders and sometimes even store owners, they are rarely viewed as individuals outside the world of men, be it brother, son, father or husband. The position of women in Bangladesh was evident even in the way women were allowed to discuss their husbands.

According to Hindu tradition, that had since been adopted by Muslims, women are forbidden to speak the name of their husbands directly—it is viewed as immodest and disrespectful. Women in Bangladesh, modesty is central to their social acceptance. From the time of birth, a Muslim woman's place in Bangladeshi society is largely predetermined. While a son is welcomed into the world with the cry of "Allah Abkar" (God is Great), a female child receives only the whisper of the Qurannic prayer. Soon after the birth of a girl, her relatives begin the negotiations for her marriage. By the age of 17, approximately 70 percent of females in Bangladesh are married, nearly all of them by an arrangement between the parents of the bride and the groom -- an arrangement which is purely practical and aimed at strengthening social ties between families.

A woman's productive value in society is equated primarily with the dowry she will bring to her husband's family. Men are responsible for earning the wages, which have become crucial for a family's survival as more and more families become landless. Even for those families with land, subsistence on the small and often unproductive plots is nearly impossible, thereby diminishing a woman's status as agricultural laborer and thus income provider, and undermining her role in society even further.

The payment of the dowry, which often occurs over the course of several years, is a significant financial burden for most families. An inability to pay severely affects a young bride's treatment in her husband's family home. In order to reverse the falling status of Bangladeshi women, international and local organizations have instituted micro-lending programs, giving women access to loans, many times as little as $75 to $125, to start their own small businesses.

Organizations such as the Grameen Bank and the Bangladesh Rural Advancement Committee (BRAC) feel that by giving poor women the means to start or expand micro-enterprise activities—buying and selling milk, sewing clothes, husking rice—a mother, wife or daughter-in-law can bring income into her household. Her productivity will increase her household status, which will likely have a significant impact on her daily life. Ashtafun Nahar, the head of a locally-based organization devoted to women's economic and social empowerment said, "Even minimal increases in a woman's ability to generate income has not only been seen to reduce the mental and physical torture of women, in many cases it has stopped altogether." While most economists agree that long-term employment provides more security and higher returns than micro-enterprise activities, traditions in Bangladesh often inhibit a woman's ability to obtain employment outside the home. Purdah, or female seclusion, is an Islamic tradition routinely practiced in Bangladesh among the Muslim majority. Purdah literally means "curtain" or "veil," but the term is used figuratively to designate the proper mode of behavior for women. Its strictest adherents are confined to their homes. When they leave, they are veiled from head to toe. This "protects" the women's modesty, while also protecting her husband's family's izzat (respectability). While denounced in the West as oppressive, many women strive to observe purdah because it increases the status of the family. Economic necessity, however, is forcing many families to abandon purdah as more than one wage-earner is often required for household survival.

Occupational purdah or the types of work considered "appropriate" and "respectable" severely restrict women forced to seek wage labor. As a result, micro-enterprise activities carried out from the home are one of the few viable options for women seeking income while also observing purdah. Most women in the rural areas are forced to sell their goods (often rice or milk) through a male wholesaler or with the help of their husbands or sons. Women are not allowed to buy or sell goods in the haats and bazaars (village markets). Although women are not usually in control of their profits, their contribution to the products sold may serve to increase their household status and earn the respect of their husbands and his family.

It is evident the status of women in Bangladesh is much lower than that of men. While poverty affects the household as a whole, women bear a disproportionate burden attempting to manage household production and consumption under conditions of increasing scarcity. Greater numbers of women than men are among the poor. The report of the Analysis of Poverty Trends Project of the Bangladesh Institute of Development Studies based on a 62 villages sample found that 76 percent of women fell under the category "poor" in terms of income and resource endowments. Women are discriminated against in intra-household allocation of resources. However, Bangladesh endorsed the Platform for Action (PFA) without any reservations and it is committed to ensuring its implementation at national level. The status of the progress in ending women's economic inequality in Bangladesh is as follows:

**Rights to Family Benefits**

Women in the government service are receiving the same family benefits as men. In fact, in some cases affirmative action has been taken in favor of women. Among the most important family benefits is the right to family housing quarters or allowances. Women married to other government servants are also entitled to their own housing allowance, even if the husband is receiving a housing allowance. In case the husband has received a housing allotment, the wife will still receive her housing alloance. The reverse is also true. While allocating government accommodation, women applicants are accorded three years seniority in the waiting list.

All other family benefits such as pensions and medical allowances are given equally to male and female employees.

Increasing Numbers and Proportion of Female Officers at All Levels:

> Considering the low percentage of female staff at all levels, the Bangladesh Government emphasizes the importance of employment and promotion of increased numbers and percentages of women at entry, mid level and particularly at senior management positions. Lateral entry of women at senior levels from within the government and on contract service from outside is emphasized. To enhance the management role and the capacity of women managers, the government stresses the need for management training and retraining.

Improving Working Conditions for Women:

> The need for improving working condition of women in service to enable them better carry out their work responsibilities is stressed. Improved working conditions include providing maternity leave, including leave during provision period, creches and day care centers, adequate numbers of separate toilet facilities, better transport facilities especially for night work and accommodation facilities for out of station tours.

Bangladesh is not a welfare state and does not provide any welfare benefits to its citizens, either men or women. However, certain service benefits are provided to government employees. These are provided equally to men and women. In addition women are given paid maternity leave. Certain special measures are being taken to accelerate the development of women.

Rights to Bank Loans, Mortgages and Other Forms of Financial Credit:

> The regular banking system with its requirements of collateral, discriminates against women since in most cases they do not own assets which can be used as collateral. Various social and cultural

customs make it difficult for women to have easy access to the banks and bank officials. They are not as familiar as men with procedures and requirements.

Some of the public or national commercial banks do have "ladies branches" but their role is more mobilization of savings than encouragement of investments. And, although it is not a legal requirement, in practice bank managers would require the consent of the husband or other male relatives, as guarantors before sanctioning loans to women.

*Plan of the government*

In March 1997 the Bangladesh Government declared the National Policy for Development of Women for the first time in its history. According to this policy, a five year plan of 1997-2002, includes the following objectives for ending women's economic inequality:

1) Achieve equality between men and women in all spheres of decision-making structure
2) Establish necessary strategy, institutional power and resources for faster development of women in all spheres of life
3) Ensure equal rights of women on land, capital and technology as well as on all economic resources
4) Reduce the gap between women and men regarding availability of necessary information, skills and knowledge to receive the economic opportunities
5) Visualize and recognize the activities of women
6) Ensure equal participation of women and men in the professional sector

*Initiatives of NGOs*

1) Develop awareness through institution building process
2) Undertake income and employment generation activities through savings and credit generation. The level of poverty in the country means that the number of women eligible to borrow from regular banks is limited. In this respect NGOs and other similar government programs that provide collateral free loans have assumed tremendous importance in providing credit to poor women. Two hundred and thirty four NGOs had

disbursed Tk.21,940 million to 3 million members up to June 1996. In view of women's greater vulnerability to poverty and the greater development and social impact obtained by providing loans to women, many programs have made it a strategy to channel all, or the major part, of the loans to women. This approach has positive implications in that it increases women's economic and financial responsibilities for their families and also increases women's access to financial resources at terms and conditions that are not exploitative, like those of informal moneylenders.

3) Undertake skill development and management training
4) Organize people and social mobilization activities for the socio-economic and political empowerment specially women of poor

***Future challenges***

1) Allocate adequate amount of money in the national budget for various women development related activities according to the proportion of women population of the country and undertake necessary initiatives to implement the plan
2) Ensure the participation of women in the main trend of development according to their representation
3) Ensure the participation of women in the decision making process according to their representation
4) Increase the opportunity of employment, investment of the state and create special structural facilities for women
5) Maintain the equal wage procedure for similar activities strictly particularly in informal sector where discrimination is pervasive
6) Provide all facilities to women laborer as per the ILO convention
7) Take necessary steps to provide bank loan to women without having to obtain the consent of the husband or other male relatives, and also without collateral
8) Ensure equal rights regarding ownership of land or resources and inheritance law (Inheritance law is discriminative against women)
9) Present education system is gender blind and a major part of it is madrasa education (religions education)

which is biased against women. It is at utmost importance to reform this education system

10) Present family law (marriage, divorce, and guardianship) is discriminatory against women

11) Major employment opportunity for women is informal sector and house-based handicrafts, small trading, vegetable gardening with micro-credit through NGO intervention. The operation mechanism does not provide any opportunity for women to go for any sustainable income generating activities. So it is important to revisit the whole system of micro-credit business.

Bangladesh Nari Progati Sangha (BNPS), so far has organized 60 thousands grassroots women. It has developed an effective linkage with civil society and these women groups for affecting advocacy and lobbying work, which is working as a linkage for policy and legal reform. It also has been successful to put pressure on NGO and civil society groups to take up the issue of good governance, secularism and democratization process as priority issue. Furthermore, BNPS is successful through its mobilization and different activism by creating different networks towards structural transformation rather then welfare and service providing for poverty alleviation to poverty eradication.

**Poverty Alleviation and Empowerment**

In recent years, micro credit programs have become increasingly popular among NGOs, donor agencies and governments. However, in reality is microcredit the panacea for poverty alleviation and does it nurture empowerment for women? In this context, most people are interested in statistical proof that women who have access to credit are more empowered as demonstrated by participation in family decisions (such as major purchase or the marriage of a child), increased fertility control, and increased health and education of children. However, all studies that attempt to assess the impact of credit programs against a control group with no credit fail to include in their data collection measures of other sources of increases in family income (such as from a child working abroad and sending home money, or a dowry due to a son's marriage). Without such measures, statistical analysis (no matter how sophisticated) cannot separate the effect of increased capital available to the family from the effect of increased capital available to the mother. Moreover, most studies measure empowerment as a function of multiple factors. These multiple factors include primarily income-related activities (activities or decisions that would not come up if the family did not have money to spend or invest.) To demonstrate, only families with extra money (regardless of the source) can decide whether to buy something or to spend money on a daughter's education. If the data set does not include families with a recent inflow of money that is not from credit, the effect of an inflow of money in the form of credit cannot be measured. Further, most studies document women's involvement or lack thereof in certain decisions.

**Microcedit and its Impact on Poverty, Well-being and Gender Equity**

Brooke Ackerly's research of three micro credit organizations in Bangladesh -Grameen, BRAC, and Save the Children - like others, could not assess the wealth/income effect of credit versus other sources of capital on empowerment. However, as a comparative study, he was able to document the differences in productive roles that women adopted as a result of participating in a credit program. Most women contributed labor to the project, meaning as a result of credit they had more work to do. For illustration, credit enables a woman to process more rice than she could without credit and to sell the processed rice in the market. Her husband may help with the labor at home, but in Bangladesh, he will most likely be the person who goes to the market to buy the unprocessed and sell the processed rice. Thus, his labor need not increase significantly, while hers does.

Women generally were not involved in the buying or selling related to their projects unless the necessary transactions could take place in local villages (baris). Finally, fewer women did the accounting for the enterprise meaning fewer women were knowledgeable about the cost of the unprocessed rice, the processed rice, and the profit of their enterprise. Thus, micro credit increased their workloads without necessarily increasing their knowledge. Importantly, there were differences in these general findings by organization. Those organizations for which empowerment of women is an expression of goal of the program, saw more women gaining market knowledge as a result of their credit. Save the Children had the greatest focus on empowerment and consequently more of its borrowers were market knowledgeable. This may be a surprising finding given that we expect local NGOs to be better at delivering locally appropriate programming than foreign NGOs, even those who employ entirely local staff. However, this finding is consistent with findings from other research. Durgam Rajasekhar and Naila Kabeer reflected on their research on a small number of microcredit programs in India (Kerala and Andhra Pradesh) and Bangladesh respectively, highlighting some of the emerging findings on empowerment. One of the common points in the two researches is that microcredit may not be the most appropriate strategy for assisting the poorest social strata. To use microcredit effectively, the borrower needs to have complementary resources, such as some land, capital, education or knowledge and experience of how to run an enterprise.

Successful borrowers were often able to rely on skills accumulated in some prior entrepreneurial experience, or on a certain level of education. This point was emphasized by Kabeer, who studied an enterprise oriented credit program - the Small Enterprise Development Project (SEDP)- that did not address itself to the poorest strata of the society. In this connection, Rajasekhar argued that some poorer women are reluctant to borrow because what they need is a facility for consumption loans not entrepreneurial activities. Hence, if microcredit is to be used as a poverty alleviation strategy for the very poor, then it needs to be more flexible in loan regulations, allowing loans for consumption. Rajasekhar's research found that one model of microcredit delivery that appeared to benefit the poorest was the self-help group. This model used microcredit as an entry point to promote empowerment. Members of self-help groups allowed to define their own rules and regulations and were obliged to rotate various roles and responsibilities among themselves. This fostered higher saving/borrowing ratios than other microcredit models because the members sustained control and ownership over group funds. The other interesting point emerging from this model was that the female members of some of these groups used their loans predominantly for "consumption" purposes, such as seeking healthcare for themselves (pregnancies) and their children's school expenses.

Besides, loans offered through the poverty-oriented microcredit programs are often too small and do not allow the borrower to undertake any viable economic activity, especially where the village infrastructure is underdeveloped. At the same time the repayment schedules, which are often on a weekly basis, put significant stress on the borrowers (women borrowers often complain of "sleepless nights"), as well as putting strain on the relationship between these women and their husbands (who may be using the loans), among the women borrowers within a group, and between the women borrowers and program officials who collect weekly installments. Ironically, the enterprise-oriented program (SEDP) in Bangladesh studied by Kabeer, which was lending to better-off individuals and those with some prior entrepreneurial experience, was giving the borrowers larger loans, monthly (as opposed to weekly) repayments, and flexible repayment. This greater flexibility may have been one of the reasons for the lack of evidence of violence in connection with microcredit in this program, which contrasted with some emerging evidence from Grameen Bank and BRAC programs, where accentuated levels of stress and violence have been reported. Kabeer's research in Bangladesh (on SEDP) suggested many women who took loans (as opposed to women who did not, or to the wives of men who took loans) reported a number of changes in their lives, which could be deemed as empowering. These changes were linked to their level of participation in the program and included: an improved sense of self due to not feeling dependent; higher levels of political activity; an improvement in their social position as their levels of assets or incomes rose; an increase in household decision making; bank accounts and land in their own names; and higher levels of investment in their daughters' education. This last finding may be seen as challenging deep-seated social norms and being truly transformative.

Finally, on the controversial issue who actually controls the loan (that is, manages the enterprise and controls the income) when women borrow, the presentations made a number of relevant observations. Referring again to women's complaints about "sleepless nights," Rajasekhar made the point that this is sometimes the result of women borrowers losing control over loan use as their husbands take over the decision-making and management of the enterprise. In some cases women prefer not to borrow from microenterprise programs because responsibility for repayment falls on their shoulders, while in the case of borrowing from village moneylenders it is their husbands who are ultimately responsible for repayment. But the evidence emerging from these programs, he stressed, was mixed. In some cases the issue of which household member controls the loan, and the income, was not of major concern to the women.

Kabeer's findings threw further light on this issue. The first point was that men who took loans were much more likely to report sole decision making (they were the main decision makers), while the women who took loans were more likely to report joint decision making. And by exploring those findings further through qualitative research it became clear that the response "joint decision making" was not a normative statement; it did actually represent a sense of being consulted in decisions regarding loan use, and of no longer being marginalized from household decision-making processes.

**Role of Women**

Even if women were not directly involved in the management of enterprise, husbands were very aware that this increased income was a product of the women having brought in the loans. But there were also a number of women who reported sole decision-making, which was unexpected in the Bangladeshi context. These cases could be divided into three groups: first, female-headed household; second, women who were regarded in the family as actually "having the brains" (a point that is often missed when one focuses on social groups and categories is that at the individual level there is often much more variation than a categorical analysis allows one to see); and third, women who were in conflict with their husbands and who used their loans to set up a "separate economy" in the household.

There is great variety in the effectiveness of credit

programs. Such variety is a function of the women who are able to borrow, their social and economic contexts, the program design of the micro credit issuing organization, and the attitudes of the grassroots workers given the responsibility of administering the loans to women. While designing studies to assess micro credit's impact on women's empowerment, one must include measures of alternative sources of income and of prioritization in decision-making if our assessments are going to have the substantive implications for empowerment we desire.

Now the question, is it possible to address income inequality and poverty by promoting micro enterprise through credit approach? If we think that poverty is the result of the global distribution of capital and the exploitation of labor, we might think that micro enterprise promotion merely brings poorer people into that system of exploitation. If credit is available, they (not the distribution of resources in their country and globally) are responsible for their own poverty. Credit may be a form of development programming that is acceptable to international lenders when other methods of development focused on health and education that may develop human capital are not.

From Rajasekhar's research findings about the self-help groups, it can be noted that one factor that is likely to jeopardize NGOs' empowerment objectives is the growing trend for the private sector to move into the field of microcredit for enterprise, purely for financial profit. Now the tension is, how to approach it? There is a definite need for ongoing monitoring of microcredit programs, but how far they are meeting their poverty and empowerment objectives?

Similarly, Kabeer's research finding also raises the issues in the direction of casualty: did microcredit empower the women borrowers, or were the microcredit programs selecting already empowered women? In the workshop, Kabeer agreed that in fact many of women who took loans were already empowered, since Bangladesh is going through many interesting changes: female education is rising and the discourse on women's rights has been very influential. But does it matter that they are already empowered? One of the biases in that system is that women have not given access to credit, and on that basis alone there is an equity and efficiency argument that they need to be given this kind of opportunity in order to exercise their suppressed entrepreneurial potential.

**Micro Enterprise**

Micro enterprise promotion through micro credit (and possibly to often unnecessarily technical assistance) should be conscious of its operating in a context of global capital, national development, and international lending. The practical implications of this more general question is: should a credit program encourage borrowers to take on increasing amounts of debt and to enlarge their enterprises, or to save capital such that they can one day self-finance? Generally, credit programs encourage savings. Those with a bank-oriented mentality encourage the borrower to keep the savings in the event that a problem with the enterprise makes it difficult to make a payment or for occasional expenditures. Another approach would be to increase borrower autonomy by encouraging borrowers to save such that they can eventually invest their own capital.

**Unleashing the Human Spirit of Women**

THP-Bangladesh is strong, expansive, deeply rooted in the principles of The Hunger Project and unequivocally committed to the end of hunger in Bangladesh. Given our strength, we are now able and committed to confront the major obstacle to achieving the end of hunger -- the severe subordination of women in Bangladeshi society

On the eve of the new millennium, we in THP-Bangladesh commit ourselves to a new phase in our work for the end of hunger: a dynamic campaign to confront and transform discrimination against women in ourselves, our organization and in the society of Bangladesh. We commit ourselves to unleashing the human spirit of women and empower women's leadership as our highest priority. The centerpiece of our strategy is to dramatically increase the number of women taking our animator training.

**Eat Last / Eat Least - a formula for poverty**

In Bangladesh, women eat last and least. They are malnourished, and give birth to children who are underweight at birth. Low birth-weight babies are permanently disadvantaged in all areas of personal development including health and mental capacity. These practices are deeply entrenched within patriarchal social customs that are sometimes justified in the name of religion - a false justification. Not only are these customs not supported by the Koran, but the essential message of Islam is the equality of all people - women and men - before God. Bangladesh pays dearly for practices that subordinate women.

Not only is the persistence of this tradition a gross violation of the dignity of women as human beings, it perpetuates the cycle of malnutrition, ill-health and poverty. Statistically, over 1/2 of the babies born in Bangladesh are underweight at birth. This compares with the percentage of underweight babies in the US of 7%, in Africa of 16% and in India of 33%. In 1990, researchers studied the impact of four types of malnutrition and undernutrition worldwide. They calculated that the loss in productivity due to low-birthweight babies amounted to a loss of 46 million years of productive, disability-free lives. The vitamin and mineral deficiencies that are suffered by these babies is equivalent to losing 5% of GNP. This loss of health and productivity is estimated to have cost Bangladesh and India together 18 billion dollars in 1995.

***Why this persists? The subordinate position of women***

To understand why this condition persists year after year, we must examine the status of women. Women are the principal providers of nourishment, both before birth and after birth. Over 60% of women in Bangladesh of childbearing age are themselves underweight and undernourished. The women suffer from mineral deficiencies and deficiencies in iodine, iron, and Vitamin A. A majority of them are anemic. A majority of them are undernourished when they are of childbearing age.

The primary reason that children are malnourished in Bangladesh is that women in Bangladesh live in a subordinated, second-class citizen position. Women and girls are more undernourished, less educated, and receive less health care than their brothers. They eat last and least. They have poor nutrition and have little additional care when they are pregnant.

Bangladesh will never achieve its full potential and the

possibility and greatness that is inherent in the Bangladeshi people." The Hunger Project is committed to this transformation as its highest priority. Joan's November visit to Bangladesh marks the start of an intensive campaign to retool and refocus the energies of The Hunger Project to make the most high-leverage difference it can to transform the subordination of women.

### *The power of the animator training in women's lives*

The centerpiece of our new strategy is to have as many women as possible take The Hunger Project's animator training, and be empowered as agents of change in their villages. The animator training is proving to be our most powerful tool for unleashing the human spirit of women in Bangladesh. In the last five years, The Hunger Project has trained 800 women as animators in its 4-day animator training. These women report a profound shift in their sense of themselves and their ability to make a difference in women's lives. Women animators have formed women's self-help groups. They have created their own enterprises and increased their own incomes. They have facilitated women to step out of their household, become literate and generate more income. They have have learned their rights - in the home and in the society. Women animators have become elected leaders in local government. They have campaigned against domestic violence and sex trafficking. They are speaking out to challenge old ideas, and create a new partnership between women and men.

### *The positive impact in men's lives*

The husbands of Hunger Project women animators report a dramatic enrichment in their own lives as a result of their wives taking the animator training. An obvious impact is the increase in family income as women establish their own entrepreneurial businesses as a result of their new found skills and leadership.

### *A new program of action*

In order to dramatically increase the number of women animators The Hunger Project is able to train and empower, we shall:

- Set high targets - increasing the number of women animators we train from hundreds per year to thousands per year.

- Rewrite the Vision, Commitment and Action Workshop and the Animator Training to provide a more in-depth examination of the condition of women, provide information on nutrition and women's rights, and make unleashing the human spirit of women the highest priority.
- Refocus the Catalyst and Hunger-Free Zone Programs to give top priority to this issue.
- Rewrite the 40-point village self-assessment protocol, to be a more potent tool for sensitizing both women and men to key issues in the development of women and girls.
- Create an Animator Empowerment program to provide regular forums for women animators to come together, learn more, organize group action and support each other as leader.
- Create an Animator Trainer Program to train more women to lead the Animator Training, in order to increase the number of animator trainings and bring them closer to women's homes.
- Create and widely disseminate a brochure in Bangla that educates people about these issues, and inspires them to transform it.
- Carry out a campaign to have Bangladesh establish a National Girl Child Day, as a day of total national mobilization for the rights and improved conditions of female children.

***Transforming Ourselves***

In support of this campaign:

- Through every forum of Hunger Project activism, both men and women in The Hunger Project will conduct their own inquiry to recognize, own and transform our own attitudes and behaviors that marginalize women, and discover a new depth of their own commitment and moral courage for this issue.
- Avoid taking any actions that unconsciously perpetuate, reinforce or acquiesce to the prevailing subordination of women in society.
- Transform our own organizational structures to "*become*

the change we seek."

- Our commitment to women's self-hood and equality requires energetic affirmative action.
- We will commit ourselves to never train more men than women, no matter how strong the demand. Far better that we devote our energies to clearing away whatever obstacles there are to increased women's participation.
- We will commit ourselves to hire an equal number of female and male staff, even if this requires extraordinary steps in staff training and development and in acquiring suitable offices.
- We will place women's leadership in the forefront of all Hunger Project activities, even if this requires mobilizing extra funds from men for a special fund to pay travel expenses of women.

The Global Office of The Hunger Project will take whatever steps are required on its part to dramatically increase worldwide support and solidarity with THP-Bangladesh in taking these historic efforts.

# 3

# Social Status

The women of Bangladesh comprise 49 per cent of the population. But their share in the economy and society lags far behind their share in the population. Traditional socio-cultural practices limit their participation and achievements in different aspects of life, which is perpetuated by archaic laws and practices of the country. Women enjoy adult franchise in Bangladesh. But they cannot exercise their voting rights in many cases because of violence religious bindings (*fatwa*), discouragement to voting long distance from polling centres and poor transport system. But despite these impediments there has been rising voter turn out in the national elections of 1996 and 2001 showing greater awareness of women voters. However, the number of women members in the 300 member parliament representation of women members in the parliament dominance of money and muscle power in politics, discouragement to participation in the name of religion by some politics, being the major factors. The government took a significant step to women empowerment by reserving one third seats for women in the local government. But the opportunity could not be translated into full realisation of power because of many factors, e.g., impediments created by male colleagues, poverty of members, insecurity of women members, circulating rumours about women members, household works, one-eyed policy of the chairman of the committee and general unsympathetic attitude towards women.

There are major differences between men and women in various aspects of socio-economic conditions. The adult literacy rate of women is only 49.5 per cent as against 67 per cent for men. Though greater progress in women education has been observed in recent years facilitated by various GO-NGO education programmes focused on women, the difference in education level between male and female has remained wide.Student enrolment in various levels of education has a pyramidal structure ¾ the number of students falling with the level of education. But the structure is more pyramidal in the case of women.The suffering and deprivation of women are glaring in the case of health and nutrition though there has been some improvement in the health status of women in recent years because of different measures undertaken in this area. The average life expectancy of women is marginally lower than that of men- 60.5 years as against 60.7 years.

Women suffer a major disadvantage in terms of access to resources and control over resources. In rural areas the most important asset is land. But the law of inheritance treats men and women differentially in terms of land distribution. The Muslim law of inheritance allows a daughter half the property of that of a son. Women under Hindu law of Inheritance are always deprived of property.

The lower or zero ownership of landed property makes access to other types of resources difficult. For examples they are less able to borrow from the formal credit market as borrowing needs collateral.The labour force participation rate of women is much lower than that of men – 50 per cent in the case of female as against 77 per cent in the case of male. The types of employment of women are different from those of men. Most women (77 per cent) are engaged in household work while most men (43 per cent) are self-employed. While 8.7 per cent of women work as paid employees, the corresponding number for men is 14.4 per cent. The differences are, to some extent, caused by the special problems faced by women in taking outside employment.

It has been observed that women suffer from wage discrimination, discrimination in promotion, lack of adequate and appropriate transport facilities, lack of child care and create facilities, burden of overtime work, night travel and night work especially in the ready made garments sector, several attacks by miscreants during travel to and from work, sexual abuse at the workplace by supervisors or bosses and lack of access to appropriate health care facilities.

Insecurity of life and property is a growing problem in Bangladesh. The problem of insecurity is, however, more acute in the case of women. They share the problems common to both men and women and suffer from some additional problems. Rape, murder, trafficking, attacks by hijackers and snatchers, street teasing, acid throwing sexual favours, etc., make life of women insecure both at home and outside home. The insecurity limits the freedom of movement of women and affects their life and occupational choices. Rape seems to be the most important form of violence to women. The physical and mental trauma suffered by the victim prevents for long period of time, and even may cause a permanent spell on the victim.

While married women suffer mostly from murder, acid throwing, physical assault, dowry, religious bindings and suicide, unmarried women suffer mostly from rape, kidnapping and trafficking, it is interesting to note that in a good number of cases the perpetrators are known persons. More importantly, in the case of murder and dowry related violence, the perpetrator is her own husband, presumably the most intimate person of her life. The backward position of women measured in terms of various socioeconomic indicators imply their worse off position in terms of poverty. There has been an increase in the number of female headed households in the country. Female headed households, are, in general, poorer than male headed households. The average income of female headed households is only 55 per cent of the average income of the poor households. Women are as a group poorest of the poor.

**Feminisation of Poverty**

The increased feminisation of poverty poses a great challenge to policy makers because GO-NGO poverty alleviation measures have demonstrated strong focus on women. Yet they failed to check the worsening poverty situation of women.

The lack of access of women to assets and resources and their general socio-economic backwardness have been responsible for such a worrisome situation. Besides, some of the benefits of the poverty alleviation measures have flowed to other members of family. In some cases, the micro-credit given to women to benefit herself, was in fact used by man. In some cases, it has been used to repay other debts or pay dowry. Such a misdirection of resource deprived women of the expected benefit of credit. In a credit starved economy where female has greater access to micro-credit than male members of the family such misdirection is probably inevitable because of the fungibility of credit. The share of women is disappointingly low in the national budget. Development projects which have direct bearing on women have received lower budgetary allocation. For example, in 2000-2001 budget, agriculture sector, where most women are engaged, has only 44 projects out of 186 projects which benefit women directly. Together, they claim 31.6 per cent of resources allocated to agriculture. The allocation in other sectors are similarly biased against women.

Women are discouraged or prevented from exercising their legal or natural rights. They are not given *moharana* (every Muslim marriage involves an agreement to pay the bride a sum of money either in cash or kind) or alimony. Women are particularly discouraged to become member of any organisation including NGOs and to work outside home.

Girls get less to eat, and poorer food than their brothers in the same age bracket, and they receive less and inferior health care. Later on they have a harder time getting into schools and learning a trade or profession, which reduces their chances of taking up a gainful occupation.

According to an assessment the International Labour Office (ILO), in the rural regions of the developing world women and girls perform three-quarters of all the jobs and produce half of the food. In return they receive only one-tenth of the total income and own less than one per cent of the means of production. In addition to their duties as housewives and mothers many women outside the farming community work in the industrial and service sectors. There, although they work as much as 25 per cent longer than men, they are paid less all along the line. These facts are abhorrent, and not only because of the injustice and the avoidable human misfortune they reflect. They also point up a problem impacting on development, in that women's earnings go preponderantly towards benefiting the family and children, whereas a considerable part of what men earn is spent first and foremost on themselves.

**New Models**

There are no universally applicable models for promoting women in developing countries. The woman's role and her social status vary not only from country to country or ethnic group to ethnic group but often from region to region as well. What does apply everywhere, however, is this: wherever women are successful financially, social recognition follows almost automatically, most notably from their husbands and male kin. Development aid projects that enable women to achieve such success thus have a catalytic effect on every other aspect of a society's development. Where socioeconomic conditions are poor, the health of the whole community is threatened. Where gender biases favour males, however, women and female children are particularly vulnerable to health risks. Simply treating a woman's state of health as a biomedical problem is thus not enough. Apart from economic and environmental conditions, a woman's health is profoundly influenced by social customs and cultural traditions. Several health problems that affect women have their roots in childhood. Due to son preference, girls suffer not only nutritional neglect, they also receive less attention during sickness than boys. According to the 1995 Human Development Report, 59 per cent of girls suffer chronic malnutrition, whereas the figure for boys is 56 per cent. The number of girls who die before the age of five exceeds that of boys by 11 per cent—which may be interpreted as preferential access to health care.

Preferential food allocation to males exacerbates malnutrition among females, who eat last and least throughout their lives. Even in their reproductive years, women appear to receive less from the family pot than men, irrespective of economic class: 77 per cent of pregnant women from middle-income households and more than 95 per cent of those from low income households weigh less than the standard of 50 kilograms. The prevalence of infection and parasitic diseases in poor communities compounds the problem.

The high maternal mortality rate of 600 deaths per 100,000 live births is the tragic evidence that also women's specific health needs suffer considerable neglect: 58 per cent of the pregnant women aged fifteen to forty-nine suffer from anaemia, and only 5 per cent of births are attended by trained health personnel according to UNDP. Moreover, those women, who are already in poorest physical shape, rarely get the rest they need, particularly during pregnancy.

A UNDP time-use study reveals that in Bangladesh a woman's work burden is 10 per cent higher than men's. It is very unlikely, especially under conditions of permanent struggles to survive and frequent child-bearing, that women can reduce their working time during pregnancy.

**Role of World Bank**

According to a World Bank Country Study, the main reasons for the high maternal mortality rate are young age and frequent pregnancies as well as the women's precarious state of nutrition—a lifetime of inadequate food intake results in insufficient growth and pelvic development for child-bearing. Between 16 per cent and 25 per cent of the maternal deaths are attributed to abortions under unhygienic conditions.

Another 20 per cent succumb to *eclampsia* (a convulsive condition during pregnancy resulting in coma and death). A further 5-10 per cent die of post-partum sepsis and the same number of tetanus. The remaining major causes are bleeding, prolonged labor, and violent deaths. A law for the protection of women against violence has been on the books since 1960. The Cruelty to Women Act of 1983 enhanced the penalties for offences against women. Although this brought needed public attention to the increasing violence against women, it has had little concrete effect because of a lack of follow-up.

UNDP's Human Development Report 1995 states that more than half of all murders of women in Bangladesh are committed by present or former partners. Especially in times of acute underemployment and economic distress, family conflicts often degenerate into violent acts against women.

The average educational level of women in Bangladesh is lower than that of men, which is itself shaky enough in comparison with other poor countries. The same applies to primary schooling. In number of school years completed, females lag far behind males especially in rural areas. Many factors have an influence on women's educational opportunities. Most studies point to poverty as the principal reason why families either fail to enrol their girls in school or withdraw them prematurely from primary school. It is not just that the direct and indirect costs of school attendance are beyond their means, but also that the children are needed at home to perform duties that fall preponderantly on the girls.

Extra income plays only a secondary role in the widespread labor demand for girls, since most of them have to work as unpaid labor: in 1990, 3.4 per cent of the girls in the age group ten to fourteen were reported as economically active.

Prevailing cultural values and norms appear to have far more significance in the low state of female education, however. Many parents in rural areas lack interest or are openly hostile to the formal education of their daughters for reasons related to social and religious norms in general and to marriage prospects in particular. The opinion is still quite widespread that education spoils a girl's character and undermines her willingness to fulfil her traditional role.

**Early Marriage**

Early marriage and the importance of preserving a girl's good reputation lead to widespread withdrawal of girls from school at puberty, especially if they attend coeducational institutions. Among other factors contributing to gender differentials in enrolments are location and physical facilities of schools, the shortage of female teachers, and a lack of basic amenities (such as latrines). Female education is further constrained by inadequate incentives (food, clothing, and scholarships) to induce the poor to send girls to school. Early marriage, which is a reflection of the low status of women and their low educational attainment, is also a social custom favouring high fertility as well as high maternal mortality. The average age at which girls marry has slightly gone up, though, from 16.4 years in 1970 to 18 years in 1990.

According to the Muslim code of religious law, girls should be wedded at puberty, which can have its onset quite early. An unmarried daughter who is beyond puberty often is still felt to be an embarrassment to the family. Since their economic value is perceived as low, girls are considered a burden on the parental home. Yet at the same time strict norms of behaviour keep them from taking up income earning work.

As a rule, the marriage is arranged by the father or

another male guardian. Bride and bridegroom do have the right to turn down a match, but it is not customary to make use of this right. Most girls are married to men who are considerably older than themselves. The age difference – averaging seven years at present -- confers an additional aura of marital authority on the husbands. The Dowry Prohibition Act of 1989 forbids the giving and accepting of a dowry under penalty of fine or even prison, but this traditional practice continues nevertheless. If the dowry does not correspond to what the bridegroom or his parents demand, the marriage pact can be broken off, in which case the family of the bride is socially disgraced.

As protection against utter destitution should she lose her husband through separation or death, under Islamic law a Bangladeshi woman can lay claim on a certain sum from him, the *mohorana*, to be given her either when she marries or in case of divorce. But this does not happen either; first, because many women are not aware of this right and second, because insisting on it would expose a woman to social censure and the risk of losing her husband's goodwill.

If a woman does demand the Mohorana in case of divorce, then her chances of remarrying plummet. In her husband's family, the wife is subordinate to all the other members of the household- females included. Her only path to social recognition is through motherhood.

Male progeny are preferred because, among other reasons, they inherit and it is their duty to provide for the elderly. Owing to the age difference among married couples, women run a high risk of being widowed, with the consequent danger of being left impoverished. In most cases they move out of their parental home without any kind of material cushion that would lend them security and independence.

**Islamic Law**

Since under Muslim law women are only inconsequentially entitled to inherit, they must depend on their sons to look after them. This fundamental dependency provides a strong incentive to women to bear as many children as possible and as early as possible as a risk insurance against abrupt poverty.

Under the constitution, both sexes have the same rights and are entitled to equal treatment under the law. Women also have the right to vote. But a low educational level, illiteracy, a feeble social and political awareness, and the duty to adhere to religious and cultural norms, all act to keep women from taking part in public life. In family matters such as marriage, divorce, guardianship for children, and rights of inheritance, most people are guided by religious laws, which discriminate quite clearly against women. Under the Islamic law of inheritance, for example, widows receive but a trifling portion of their husband's estate, most particularly if there are no children or only daughters. In the absence of a son as male heir, most of the estate passes to the male relatives of the deceased. This law gives women another strong motivation to bear many children. As a rule the wife waives the right to the share (minuscule in any case) due her by law from her husband or parents so as not to jeopardise her chances of assistance in case of acute emergency.

The overwhelming majority of women in rural Bangladesh, not only live in grinding poverty but are also exposed to the brunt of the dilemma presented by religious culture and tradition on the one hand and growing poverty as a by-product of landlessness on the other. The behaviour that the Muslim faith expects of women is encoded in Purdah - the moral obligation of the woman to live in seclusion, in submission and with modesty. In Bangladesh Purdah is manifested as the strict limitation of women's mobility outside their homestead (*bari*). Women who leave their homestead and enter the public male domain must dress so that body and face are covered. Not to do so would be held a provocative and public offence and would blemish the family's repute. The segregation of the sexes makes the labor market virtually off limits to women.

In 1993, the female share of the labour force was a mere 8 per cent. Observance of Purdah earns high social and religious prestige, but only the more affluent can afford to stick strictly to the rules. Men work primarily as agricultural labourers or producers; they are likewise responsible for the selling of agricultural produce and for purchases on the markets. Women, in contrast, are restricted to activities that can be performed within their homestead, as for example, the preparation of foods that are sold in the village or at urban markets as finished products, small livestock keeping, and handicrafts such as spinning, weaving, or needlework. The advantage of such extremely low-paid at-home work is that it collides least with a woman's duties as housewife and mother and with the prescriptions of *purdah*. The isolation of the woman thus kept busy puts the seal on her powerlessness and ensures male dominance. For reasons of respectability women are not allowed to trade in public. Normally it is the men who bring the product to market and transact business. Often, however, it is also pre-pubescent girls or post menopausal women, who do not yet or no longer pose a danger to society.

With acute poverty on the increase, however, women are being forced more and more to venture into male domains. The gradual opening of the labour market for them is a two-edged sword, however. Purdah remains so powerful a normative code of proper conduct that manual labor in public brings women appreciable loss of status, exposing them to psychic stress and insecurity. The reputability of the whole family hinges on the «invisibility» of the woman.

Her work in road construction and similar work sectors is a sign of great poverty and desperation—otherwise women would not take on such jobs. The other side of the coin is the opportunity for social change resulting from the emergence of women from their traditional condition of dependence.

**Female Labour**

The reason for the growing popularity of female labor is not difficult to guess: under the pretence that their weaker physical constitution makes them much less productive they are as a rule paid notably less than men: The average wage for women's non-agricultural labor stands at 42 per cent of the average wage for men. The ratio of female wages to male wages is likely to be even lower in rural labor sectors.

Under the rigid rules defining the place and role of the sexes in rural Bangladesh, women are fettered by the contradictions of their purdah-dictated status, which sharply curtails their entitlement to productive resources and even their own labor, while the men's obligation to protect and support the women is governed by normative control. So whereas women's traditional duties continue to be valid unchanged, their normative entitlements are being worn away by advancing relativism, a process that spreading poverty makes particularly acute. It is no surprise that in a social environment such as this, women have scant chance of surviving in a way befitting human dignity.

Rather it is determined by the individual's place in the family hierarchy, which depends in turn on age, sex and relationship to the household head. This traditional asymmetry in satisfying basic needs translates under condition of absolute poverty into a higher incidence of illness and mortality among women and girls. Women's institutionally limited access to resources and their excessively high dependence on normatively codified entitlements produce specifically gender-linked differences in the process of impoverishment.

The increasing number of households headed by women is a further indication of how normative entitlements are eroding. More and more men from the poor strata no longer earn enough to provide for their families. Many leave home for a time or even for good to seek work in the cities. Seasonal divorces are the result, particularly in periods of acute food scarcity. For women, then, the impoverishment process proceeds along several tracks. They become poorer along with the rest of the family, and through the breakdown of the household and the attendant loss of their normative entitlements.

Over the years, various women's organisations, NGO's, civil society, and human rights activists have contributed significantly towards achieving positive changes in reducing discrimination against women. A major portion of the political constituency keenly observes the commitments made by political parties to eliminate discriminations against women. There are two main objectives of this policy brief.

i) Pinpoint the link between discrimination against women, women's empowerment and national development.
ii) Obtain from political parties a clear mandate for remedying existing inequalities between women and men.

This brief highlights that discrimination against women

hits not only the fundamental human rights of women but is also detrimental to economic growth and prosperity of the country. Women are more than 90 per cent of the workers in the garment industry, which is the most important foreign exchange earner of the country. Women also contribute to 50 per cent production in agriculture sector. They are in the construction sector and small trade and business. A large number of women also works in informal sectors and in domestic service. Women are also participating in various professions. They are overcoming various obstacles and becoming doctors, engineers, educators, accountant and bankers and also joining governmental and non-governmental services.

**In Progress of Nation**

Thus women are actively contributing to the progress of the nation. Beyond their significant economic contribution women also work 10 to 18 hours a day in the household sector preparing food, caring for children, fetching water and sources of cooking energy etc, which are financially non-remunerative. They also perform the duty of providing care for the sick and elderly in the house and also in the community.

Women provide pre-school and regular education and also spend time with the children and help to develop their social skill and value system. These are essential activities, which help the social and economic system to function smoothly. Women perform these roles and responsibilities under most difficult situations and face adversity in all possible manners. Women are willing and able to extend their roles and contributions to the society if a favourable environment can be created. Therefore, women and human right partners demand equal rights and equitable treatment and opportunities for women. The straightforward computation is that:

i) if political parties want votes, they must understand the needs of the women and respond to those needs.
ii) They must recognise where the inequalities between women and men are and what the political, economic and social consequences of those inequalities are. And
iii) the election manifestoes put forward by each political party must clearly state its position on women's needs

and lay down specific pledges for fulfilling those needs within a specified time.

Women's organisations have been for a long time demanding actions to be taken to reduce and eventually eliminate all kinds of discriminations against women so that women and men have equal rights, opportunities and responsibilities in all spheres of life. As a result, government and other development partners have started to pay more attention towards achieving equality between women and men. In this respect, during recent years, the government has taken a number of actions. For example, such as the Bangladesh became a signatory to the Beijing Declaration and endorsed its Platform for Action (PFA). Formulated a national policy for the advancement of women. Established the Ministry of Women and Children Affairs to act as a facilitator and catalyst in implementing, coordinating, and monitoring of WID programmes. It established a 44 member National Council for Women's Development (NCWD) chaired by the Prime Minister, in 1997. Adopted of a National Action Plan (NAP). It withdrew some reservations to the CEDAW (Convention on the Elimination of All Forms of Discrimination against Women) and undertook affirmative actions for selection of women in the public sector and elected bodies.

Bangladesh is one of the poorest countries in the world. With a per capita GNP of US$ 350, Bangladesh ranks 175 among 206 countries in the World Development Report (WDR) 1999, of the World Bank. In the WDR Bangladesh ranks 147 among 174 countries in Human Development Index and ranks 140 among 160 countries according to the Gender Development Index (GDI). These facts are no coincidences and they indicate the linkage between poverty and discrimination against women. The objective of attaining growth and reducing poverty is consistent with the objective of attaining equality between women and men. Various micro studies indicate that:

i) The 'hard-core' poor are largely women.

ii) Women are more susceptible to becoming poor when they lose the male earning member of the family due to abandonment, divorce, or death.

iii) Because they face social barriers in accessing economic assets, it is much harder for women to overcome poverty.

The reduction of poverty is impossible without addressing the issue of discrimination against women.

Various indicators show that women are facing discriminations. In health, indicators of child mortality, high maternal mortality, life expectancy and household expenditure distribution manifest systemic discrimination against women. In education also the women are behind men. Dowry demand, dowry related violence and death in the households have become endemic. Bangladesh ranks as one of the countries with the highest number of trafficking in women and children. Women are also subject to discrimination due to inconsistent application of laws. In matters related to citizenship the current statutory laws do not allow a Bangladeshi woman to transmit her citizenship to her children or spouse. In politics also women have no voice in decision making.

Women of Bangladesh consist of diverse groups. There are inequalities among them. However, discriminations against women exist in all spheres of life and among women in different regions of the country, religions, ethnic, social, cultural, religious, regional, and economic groups. These discriminations manifest themselves in different degrees and forms among women with different background. However, the common concern against discrimination arises from the fact that discrimination against women leads to their disempowerment, which in turn leads to further discriminations against them.

These discriminations are eventually translated into the fact that women are not part of decision making at home and other spheres of lives and have very little control over their own lives. Therefore, empowering women is essential for eliminating discrimination against them in all social strata. The local organisations and NGOs have emerged with a new generation of ideas to fight against poverty and gender inequality existing in the country. Various kinds of women's organisations work in Bangladesh. The traditional women's organisations has been focusing on delivering such as women's education and health service. However, this approach has been inadequate to address the strategic needs of the women.

NGOs in Bangladesh do not only see women's economic empowerment as its goal, but encourages uniting of the poor women in groups as part of a larger struggle. If the programmes are undertaken collectively they are more likely to achieve their goals than otherwise.

Credit based income generating activities are the main tasks for most of the NGOs. Credit programmes can be a means to women's empowerment. Credit programmes begin by organising poor rural women into small groups. The group formation among the women helps generating peer group support and solidarity. Through meetings the awareness process starts. After selecting a specific income generating project they are given training.

The concept of time and regularity becomes important as a strict discipline with weekly savings are established. Issue-based meetings is a forum where each credit group member must participate, they chose issues which are important to their lives such as immunisation of children, family planning, school issues, legal issues etc. The money borrowed from the NGO helps them raise their position towards their husband and other house hold members, and their self-confidence is increased. As a result their practical needs are largely fulfilled and their strategic needs are recognised by the family and the community, as both their conditions and positions begin to change. The credit programmes have a visible impact on the women's empowerment. The women's bargaining position in the home increases as they enhance their economic contribution to the family. The strength of earning an income together with the strength of belonging to a group help women establish new roles for themselves. However, there may also be threats, such as if the women hand over the money to their husbands they may be more dependent of the husbands, and gender inequality will be reinforced.

The NGOs also provide non-economic support, such as health care, non-formal primary education, family planning in addition to the skill training. The non-economic support also help organising the group formation for the credit program. The governmental formal education often helps to reinforce the women's domestic role and does not bring about any change in social relations either within or outside the family. The non-formal education run by the NGOs on the other hand seeks to promote consciousness among the women about gender inequality so that women not only understand the causes of their oppression but also take steps to improve their conditions.

Multi-dimensional difficulties and constraints have been encountered in the work for women's empowerment. Most of the violence towards women in Bangladesh take place within the households. The reported cases of violence are increasing. There are two reasons are given below:

i) All the increased awareness of violence against women has facilitated uncovering occurrence of violence.

ii) Rural women are at a crossroad now and have been faced with the ideology of patriarchy which help reinforce the power hierarchies within the family.

The increasing trend of violence against women should therefore be explained as the outcome of a contradiction against the ideology of patriarchy, manifested in social restrictions against women's mobility, the system of early marriage for girls, restriction on negotiation rights etc. A classic case of patriarchy is the assumption that the male must exercise control over women by limiting her mobility to the home. Such control of female sexuality is further elevated by creating an image of the mother as divine and women who do not live up to the ideal, as 'fallen women'.

In fact the family is the breading grounds for some of the most persistent discrimination against women, such as sexual subordination of women, restriction of the mobility of women and different access to resources within the family. The NGOs are still facing difficulties when trying to convince the women that gender inequalities are not natural but a social construction. The issue of contraceptive use is well researched in Bangladesh. The engagement of women in credit group activities and empowerment are positively linked with the use contraceptives. The success of increasing the use of contraceptives in Bangladesh in spite of the lack of economic development was made possible through the massive door-to-door supply service that has been provided throughout the country. This programme may itself have had a consciousness raising effect on the rural population.

When the contraceptive knowledge is universal and the social costs to use contraceptives has been reduced it has led to a rise in use of contraceptive. If the development programmes tackle the sources of subordination, provide access to information, help women to gain self esteem and ability to control their own affairs, they will increase the possibilities of creating a context in which use of contraceptives will rise. The credit empowerment process addresses the structural problems as the power relations change and the women's bargaining situation improves. The social context of the rural women has been changing as the economic life has become more complex. The women engaged in self-help projects and credit groups have managed better in the new situation. Many of them have accepted that the use of contraception can be economically beneficial as fewer children are born. Women's growing sense of self respect and bargaining capacity within the household may have diminished the men's resistance towards contraceptives. Women's reproductive rights and empowerment goes together. Increasing the status of women also enhance their decision-making capacity, especially concerning sexuality and reproduction. This is essential for the long-term success of the population programmes. It is also important to increase access to health service to succeed with the programmes. Both these facts have now been recognised by government.

Even though most of the NGOs in Bangladesh do not directly provide health services they contribute greatly through promoting the messages that women should have control over their own body and the right to decide over when and how many children they should have. The participation in such programmes by poor women may lead to a dynamic process social development with increased empowerment and self confidence. Early programmes for women's empowerment failed as they overlooked the structural factors that perpetuated the oppression and exploitation. The fulfilment of practical needs such as food, health care and education can not empower women unless the long-term strategic needs are met. The process of empowerment requires transformation of structures of subordinance, control over material and intellectual resources, gaining decisions, making authority and reduction of gender inequality.

### (ICEDAW) Women in Bangladesh Demand Equal Rights to Property

When it comes to property, both majority Muslims and

minority Hindus in Bangladesh discriminate against women. Under the Muslim law of inheritance, a daughter is eligible to only half the share of property given to a son while Hinduism does not specify her share.

Women's rights groups have been demanding equal rights to property, and also a uniform family code in Bangladesh to give women rights to property, marriage, divorce, guardianship of Childred, and other things.

The Constitution treats each citizen fairly. It declares "the state shall not discriminate against any citizen on grounds of religion, race, caste, sex or place of birth".

Prominent lawyer Salma Khan, chairperson of the U.N. convention on the Elimination of All Forms of Discrimination Against Women (CEDAW) Committee believes women in patriarchal Bangladesh suffer injustices from birth.

Islamic laws, she argues, are not the only obstacle to equality before law, because inheritance has been made a subject of civil courts in other Muslim countries like Egypt, Tunisia and Nigeria.

"There is no doubt that in doing so some obstacles must be faced, but the government and all concerned have to move forward with firm determination," she said.

But Bangladesh Law Minister Abdul Matin Khasru said his government is committed to affirmative action for women, "but it is not possible for a democratic government to take a step that might hurt the religious faith of the people".

Asked if this meant that inheritance laws would never change in women's favor, he skillfully side-stepped the question by saying that first people have to be prepared to accept change before a decision is taken.

Discrimination against women is ingrained in society. When a son is born, 'azan' or blessings are called out by the mullahs in mosques, while the family mourns the birth of a daughter.

A girl is taught from childhood that virtue lies in sacrifice. She is taught to be subservient, and to endure all oppression in silence. Self-esteem is not deemed a virtue.

A woman who eats last and least and quietly takes all the abuse from her husband is considered an ideal woman, particularly in rural Bangladesh.

Women in the villages work longer and harder than menfolk, caring for domestic animals, in the fields, tending children, and cooking. All the boiling, drying and husking of paddy is exclusively women's work.

Hours spent in household activities like caring for elderly relatives and the sick are not seen as work since they do not earn money for the family.

As farm labour, women get roughly 40 per cent of a man's wage, according to researchers.

Dr Atiar Rahman, a research fellow of the Bangladesh institute of Development Studies (BIDS), has calculated in a recent study that women work 21 hours more in a week than men.

Similarly the U.N. children's agency, UNICEF, estimates that boys who do not go to school spend only 12 minutes on house work daily, while girls who have dropped out shoulder five hours of work around the work.

As a result of her work load and child bearing responsibilities, women age much faster than men, and suffer from anemia and other problems related to nutrition deficiency.

Take Mariam who works as a domestic in a home in the capital city. She is worn out after having three children in four years, but her husband and his family refuse to consider family planning options because they want a boy.

Equal property rights for daughters would go a long way in raising their social status, rights activists campaigning for an end to gender discrimination feel.

Lawyer Sigma Huda of the Bangladesh Society for Implementation of Human Rights refuses to believe the discrimination between men and women is sanctioned by religion.

Reforming the Muslim inheritance laws would not clash with personal laws, she insists. "It must be remembered that the Muslim Family Laws ordinance of 1961 was passed establishing different issues which are implied and not supported by the Holy Koran,"she says.

Also, the Bangladesh Constitution of 1972, which assures women equality, has coexisted with the Shariah Laws, even though they contradict each other, points out Farida Akhter, a well-known rights activists.

Ensuring daughters have the legal right to an equal share of parental property would conform with the fundamental rights of the Constitution, and the government has an obligation to fulfill the right, she said.

**Introduction**

One of the most important women's groups in Bangladesh is Women for Women: A Research and Study Group, located in Dhaka. It is a pioneer non-government , non-profit, voluntary women's organization, engaged in research and public education programmes on gender issues with a view to enhancing the status of women. It was established in 1973 by a group of committed woman professionals, representing a variety of academic disciplines. The Group strongly felt the need for developing a sound information base for identifying the issues relating to the disadvantaged status of women in Bangladesh and for creating public awareness with a view to ameliorating the existing situation. Since then, Women for Women has been engaged in research, information, dissemination, advocacy awareness and motivational programmes. The objectives of Women for Women are :

1. To create awareness among people of Bangladesh, particularly policy planners and public functionaries, about the need for enhancing women's status and molding public opinion for action against the oppression and exploitation of women.
2. To organize, undertake and promote research and study in all areas of women's life in general, and to focus on the specific problems impeding their integration in development efforts in particular, keeping in view the national priorities.
3. To be a forum for effective advocacy for gender equity through dissemination of policy-oriented research findings concerning women through publications, research, seminars and exchange forums.
4. To inform and educate a wider audience about critical issues, current concerns and to promote interaction through publications and national conventions.
5. To establish and develop linkages and networking with similar groups at home and abroad.

6. To create and develop gender-sensitivity among planners, public functionaries, development agency personnel and programme implementors through relevant gender training programmes.
7. To extend cooperation and consultancy services to the government as well as to other national and international agencies involved in the area of women and development.

Bangladesh Human Rights Commission is a voluntary organisation. It was established in the year 1987. It is an affiliated member of OMCT , International Commission of Jurists, and International Association of American Minorities. It also has accredited status with the UNO. BHRC is the largest Human Rights Organization in Bangladesh. It deals with various activities to upkeep Human Rights situation.

Followings are some of many : Legal Aid Programme for Victims of Torture; Medical Aid Programme for Victims of Torture; Legal Literary and Publication Programme; Investigation and fact finding Programme Protecting Minorities and Tribal Rights Programme; Research Programme; urgent Action Programme; Legal Training Programme; Legal Training Programme; Election Monitoring Programme; Disaster Management Programme.

I shall restrict myself to the violation of Human Rights against women, the type of torture they suffer, the legal framework in the country and the activities of BHRC to help them in the relevant fields.

Bangladesh is a country with a population of about 140 million. The per capita income is about 363 Dollars. But more than 50 per cent people live below poverty line.

The women are considered 2nd class citizens. Though various laws and Acts have been made to protect them, they are easy prey to persecution, torture and injustice.

The injustice is imposed socially and by religion.

**Type of Torture**

1. Women fall prey to Acid Burn, inflicted upon them by male perpetrators. Usually the criminals do this after being refused to have sexual relations or proposal of marriage. Sometimes the cause is for acquiring her property or dowry from her parents.

2. Women are sometimes burnt to death by the husband or his family for the sake of dowry. Usually dowry is taken during the marriage. But the greedy family puts pressure on the family of the girl for further dowry and in case of failure, resort to such barbaric activities. Sometimes, in order to get rid of torture, the women commit suicide.

**Social Injustice**

The birth of a female child is rarely considered a happy incident. If a woman cannot have a male child, usually the husband remarries.

The female child is also given less priority. They are given less love and affection by the family and the relatives.

Female child is usually offered less nutritious food, less money is spent on their education. They are more abused and rebuked. They have to do large part of the household work.

**Discrimination by Religion**

1. The Hindu women cannot inherit father's property.
2. The Daughter inherits ½ that of the brother by Muslim Family Law, If a person dies without leaving a male child, ½ his/ her property goes to his/her brother and the daughter only inherits ½ of his/her property but in case only a male child is heir he inherits all of the property.
3. In the eyes of "Shariat Law" a woman is considered ½ that of a man. In "Shariat Law" 4 witnesses are always necessary. But in case women are witnesses double number is necessary. Again if only women are witnesses, the case is disregarded.

**Women Trafficking**

Thus we see that the women are victim of social and religious injustice. They are brought up in an environment of unfriendliness. Then again, the women fall prey to kidnapping. They are kidnapped and sold to different brothels. They are also trafficked illegally to other country like India, Pakistan and Middle East. Several type of such trafficking is there.

1. *Through marriage* :Sometimes some male perpetrator get married to woman and take them out of the village, (Parents' home) and bring her to the town. There he engages her and forces her to do immoral activities. Sometimes she is sold to brothels or other countries.

2. *Through Kidnapping* : Female children are kidnapped and are forced to do immoral act or are sold out.
3. Sometimes the female village teenaged girls or middle-aged women are lured to get jobs in the cities. They believe and come to the cities only to find that they have been brought to work as prostitutes or sold to foreign countries.
4. Sometimes they are sent to the foreign country as Garments labour or other office-worker. But after reaching the country they find that they have to work as housemaids or prostitutes.

Mr. Chairman, Bangladesh has a well-developed set of National laws. In addition to its Penal Code, Bangladesh has passed some other laws to address specific needs of women in the country. So far the willingness of the Government and also the opinion of the members of the legislature is concerned, the women are well cared for and actions are "Meant " to be taken to reduce cruelty to women.

But in reality everything is meaningless. The following is a narration of the reason. The legal procedure in Bangladesh is very lengthy. At first a crime is to be reported to the local police station. About 95 per cent police officers are thoroughly corrupt. The women usually cannot pay any bribe. And actually they are the victims so question of paying bribe does not arise at all.

But they have to make the local police officers "HAPPY" in order to file the complain and get a well documented "Charge Sheet" written. Usually the offender is more powerful. They make the police officer "HAPPY" and gets a "Charge Sheet" which is so inaccurate, vague and under rated that it does not stand when put up in the court.

Again after a sentence is passed in the lower court it goes to the session Judge Court and then to the High Court and ultimately to the Supreme Court. The process takes in excess of 2 to 3 years at the least. 90 per cent women or their families can not bear the cost of the lengthy legal procedure.

The perpetrators usually remain at large on bail and persecute the victims and their family to withdraw the case. Sometimes they burn their houses or even kill or injure other members of the family. Till now we have more than 1000 acid victims cases and only in 13 cases sentences have been passed. These too are in the lower courts only. So where comes the justice? How can we prevent cruelty to the women? Should we wait for the perpetrators to throw acids on women and we shall treat them only ?No!! The perpetrators must be brought to justice so that the crime in itself is lowered and we have less case to deal with.

As if all these are not enough. It is a shameful thing to say that even many judicial members are corrupt and sometimes the judgement can be bought.

So in order to prevent the women from suffering and falling prey to the Acid Burn, the legal procedure must be effective.

BHRC proposed to the Government to set up Special Tribunals which may be headed by a judge of the High Court and the judgement passed may only be appealed to the Supreme Court. If such Tribunals are made the criminals can be brought to justice.

BHRC appeals to the International Community to put all its power to persuade the Government of Bangladesh to take up effective measures to give justice to the suffering thousands. Hundreds of young women in Bangladesh are being attacked with Acids. At least 20 cases of Acid Burn occur every month and the victims are almost always women and children.

Sulfuric acid is the commonest used. It melts away skin and muscle; often to the bone. Steps and are being taken to restrict the selling of acid but it is virtually impossible, as it is a common requirement in the battery repair shop and tannery industries.

Acid throwing increased about 7 years ago coincided with a new thrust by women in Bangladesh to assert their rights. With the help of the "Micro-Credit" programme started by various NGO's there have been uplifts in the condition of the women. They have grown self honour and independence and refuse to be a commodity in the hand of the father or the husband. It may be reasoned that acid throwing is a tragic by product of a gender revolution.

Again, 80 per cent of the female if arrested by the police for various reasons, fall prey to the carnal desire of the police officers. Last year 16 such cases were reported.

Bangladesh Human Rights Commission has taken up the matter of Acid Burn very seriously. In case of Acid Burn victims, as soon as a case is reported, the local members of the organization goes to the family of the victim. They give them psychological support, take up the matter to the police, provide initial medical treatment by the local doctors and ultimately bring the victim to Dhaka. The Organisation has a hospital there in Dhaka where the victim is treated by Surgeons, Plastic Surgeons, Ophthalmologist and other relevant specialists.

BHRC does the necessary follow up with the local police station. The police officers are deterred to the recourse of corruption. Presently BHRC is giving legal assistance to about 200 Acid Burn cases and is giving medical aid to about 60 victims.

BHRC has involved itself in giving legal assistance to all the atrocities caused against women while in police custody. BHRC also gives legal assistance to the women who became victims if torture by their husband.

BHRC has given legal aid to some women who were trafficked out of the country. About 123 women were found in India who were brought back to Bangladesh.

About 6000 women were trafficked out of border every year. The task of recovering them, bringing them home and rehabilitate them is a mammoth task.

All conscious people of the world must work side by side to help out these poor victims.

As per Article 28 of our Constitution, it is obligatory for the state to make provisions for betterment of the women and children and the neglected section of the society. Under Article 25 (6), Universal Declaration of Human Rights, every child is entitled to special care, treatment, social security whether born of wed lock or not. Again under UN convention on the Rights of Children, the state is responsible for sound upbringing of children. The convention enjoins principally the ways that adults and governments must adopt to protect the children, support their health, education and development. It also includes the right to have home, food and also right to protection from abuse and neglect.

But in our country the girl child remains neglected, undesired in the family and unwanted in the society. Once upon a time the girl child was buried alive. The lives of many female children are shattered by extreme poverty and discrimination in terms of facilities and social protection.

We have no birth registration system as a result a large number of female children, teen-aged girls, women are trafficked within the territory and out of border. The same reason complicates their rescue, release and repatriation. And even after their rescue and repatriation, their reintegration in the society and family is far more difficult due to social taboos and brutal customs.

Prostitution is an immoral act. It is very degrading. The extent of suffering can only be understood by the victim. More than 25 per cent girls working in different brothels are under the age of 18 years. 95 per cent of those girls are trafficked under the age of 18 and about 25 per cent are under the age of 12. In the World Summit for children in 1990, governments pledged to give every child a better life and promising future. They signed the World Declaration on the survival, protection and development of children and a Plan of Action for implementing the World Declaration.

As BHRC is a powerful organization with powerful men in it, the perpetrators of crimes against women are more aware and careful than before. They know that there will be BHRC against any victim and thus the victims are nowadays not an easy prey. As I told you before, this sort of crime is usually committed against the poor as they have limited resources to fight back, with the help of BHRC, nowadays the victims are no more women of the poor sect. BHRC never let go a crime unchallenged. If the legal proceedings would have been shortened and the criminals were duly punished, the incidence of this and other barbarian crimes committed against women, would be greatly reduced.

People from all walks of life must come forward to help fulfill the World Declaration. Only observance of World Children Day, etc. will not solve the problem but the all out effort of the Government and people and the help of the Developed Countries will ensure the well-being of the destitute children of LDCs.

I, on behalf of Bangladesh Human Rights Commission like to implore upon the International Community to come forward and strengthen the hands of BHRC with the help of other Human Rights Activities, in home and aboard, we are positive that good result will definitely be obtained.

Ladies and gentlemen, I take the pleasure to thank Mr. Saiful Islam Dildar, Secretary General, BHRC to give me a chance to present the woeful condition of the women in my country. And thank you all present here for giving a patient hearing.

**Law for Muslim Women in Bangladesh**

The legal status of the Muslim women in Bangladesh is defined by the principles of Sharia through Muslim personal law along with the general law which is non-religious and secular in its character. The Muslim personal law covers the field of marriage, divorce, maintenance, guardianship of children and inheritance whereas the general law covers the rights under the Constitution, penal codes, the civil and criminal procedure codes, evidence act, etc. It is necessary to examine the legal status of the Muslim women in Bangladesh in the context of these two sets of law as in both cases women are supposedly fortified with theoretical legal rights, but there is a gulf of difference existing between theory and its actual application. Most important of all, it must be seen that some of these laws though excellent in theory prove largely elusive in practice. The main hurdle that lies in the way of the practical application of the legal rights of women in Bangladesh is obviously the inherent contradiction of attitude that permeates the male oriented society considerably supported by religious beliefs. In this discussion, however, I shall mainly refer to those statutes or those provisions of a statute which treat men and women differently. Matters not covered herein after should be understood to have egalitarian principles giving women the same rights and obligations as the men. Let us discuss the legal rights of Muslim women in Bangladesh under the following heads :

1. Succession and right to property
2. Marriage, divorce and connected matters
3. Maintenance
4. Guardianship of children, and

5. Fundamental rights.

Before going onto specific rights we must know that the large majority of people in Bangladesh are Muslims and of these most are Hanafi Muslims while an only small minority of them belong to any other sects. Thus in general when a point is made about the law relating to Muslims it will be referring to the law which governs the majority. Therefore, we should note that historically the provisions we regard as provisions of pure Islamic Law are to a large extent Quranic utterances which were applied to the reformation of the pre-Islamic Arabian customary law. (Salma Sobhan, p. 10). According to Fyzee, "The Koranic reform came as a super-structure upon the ancient tribal laws: it corrected many of the social and ancient tribal laws: it corrected many of the social and economic inequalities then prevalent." Fazlur Rahman also makes the same point, "Whereas the spirit of the Quranic legislation exhibits an obvious direction towards the progressive embodiment of the fundamental human values... nonetheless the actual legislation of the Quran had party to accept the then existing society as a term of reference." We should also note fürther that these laws in the sub-continent have been modified in many cases not only by Statute and by custom but also by case law. The other important point to remember is that though Quran has immensely improved the status of women in several directions, society as a whole maintained the inequalities that still remained. Not only that, though over the course of years some disparities were modified by different laws, custom has sometimes been strong enough to militate against the Quranic rule of law. There is, therefore, no reason to suppose that all the rules that we are going to consider were meant to be definitive for all times. Now let us return to the specific laws.

**1. Succession and Right to Property**

Muslim law of inheritance has two distinct elements, namely, the customs of ancient Arabia and the rules laid down by the Quran and Prophet Mohammad. Under the customary law of pre-Islamic Arabia the women in whatever capacity were excluded from inheritance. The Quran made quite a considerable change of the position.

According to the Muslim Law there are three kinds of

heirs (i) "sharers" who are entitled to a prescribed share of the inheritance, (ii) "residuaries" who take on prescribed share, but succeed to the residue left after satisfing the claims of the sharers, and (iii) "distant kindreds" who are blood relations other than the sharers and residuary, and succeeded generally in the absence of sharers and residuries. In the classification of the heirs, it is important to note that though the son's son and son's daughter have been made residuary and sharer respectively, daughter's children have been made distant kindreds. The principles of succession among the sharers and residuaries are two-fold, (i) The nearest in blood relationship excluded the remote one and (ii) Whoever is related to the deceased through any person shall not inherit while the person is living.

Under the Muslim Law, the wife (or wives taken together) get one-eighth if there is child, and one-fourth if there be no child from the estate of her husband, though the husband gets exactly double. Mother gets from the estate of her sons one-sixth when there is child of her son or when there are two or more brothers or sisters or one brother and one sister f her son, and one third when there is no child and not more than one brother or sister of her son. On the other hand, the father gets from the estate of his son one-sixth if there be child of his son, he gets the entire residue after satisfying other sharers claim, and so on and so forth. It is significant that the Quran has provided that daughter, mother and wife would under all circumstances be entitled to some share in the inheritance and are not liable to exclusion from inheritance, but they are not treated at par with their male counterparts, i.e., son, father and husband and to this extent rules of inheritance are discriminatory. Women in fact were not given parity in the matter of their shares and as a general rule, the female is given one-half the share of the male. Salma Sobhan writes, since "the Koran is to be likened to an "amending act" rather an exhaustive code.. in the changed society there is little reason to perpetuate this distinction." The case of sister's inheritance is equally discriminatory. According to the rule of nearer in relationship excluding the remoter in relationship, children of a pre-deceased son or daughter would not inherit if a person died leaving another son. This often rendered the child or child of pr-deceased child destitute. This inequity, however, has been removed by Muslim Family Laws ordinance, 1961 which provides that the children of the pre-deceased child would inherit the share which the pre-deceased children would have inherited had he or she been alive. But the widow of a predeceased son remains as helpless as before as she does not inherit anything of this ordinance.

**2. Marriage, Divorce and Connected Matters**

Marriage in Islam is a contract and every Muslim of sound mind who has attained puberty may enter into a contract of marriage. Puberty is presumed, in the absence of evidence, when one reaches the age of 15 years, but this presumption is reputable.

**Women's Health and Nutritional Security in Bangladesh**

Where socio-economic conditions are poor, the health of the whole community is threatened. Where gender biases favour males, however, women and female children are particularly vulnerable to health risks. Simply treating a woman's state of health as a biomedical problem is thus not enough. Apart from economic and environmental conditions, a woman's health is profoundly influenced by social customs and cultural traditions.

Many of the health problems that affect women have their roots in childhood. Due to son preference, girls suffer not only nutritional neglect, they also receive less attention during sickness than boys. According to the 1995 Human Development Report, 59 per cent of girls suffer chronic malnutrition, whereas the figure for boys is 56 per cent . The number of girl who die before the age of five exceeds that of boys by 11 per cent which may be interpreted as preferential access to health care.

Preferential food allocation to males exacerbates malnutrition among females, who eat last and least throughout their lives. Even in their reproductive years, women appear to receive less from the family pot than men, irrespective of economic class: 77 per cent of pregnant women from middle-income households and more than 95 per cent of those from low income households weigh less than the standard of 50 kilograms. The prevalence of infection and parasitic diseases in poor communities compounds the problem.

The high maternal mortality rate of 600 deaths per 100,000 live births is the tragic evidence that also women's specific health needs suffer considerable neglect : 58 per cent of the pregnant women aged fifteen to forty-nine suffer from anaemia, and only 5 per cent of births are attended by trained health personnel according to UNDP. Moreover, those women, who are already in poorest physical shape, rarely get the rest they need, particularly during pregnancy. A UNDP time-use study reveals that in Bangladesh a woman's work burden is 10 per cent higher than men's. It is very unlikely, especially under conditions of permanent struggles to survive and frequent childbearing, that women can reduce their working time during pregnancy.

According to a World Bank Country Study, the main reasons for the high maternal mortality rate are young age and frequent pregnancies as well as the women's precarious state of nutrition—a lifetime of inadequate food intake results in insufficient growth and pelvic development for childbearing. Between 16 per cent and 25 per cent of the maternal deaths are attributed to abortions under unhygienic conditions. Another 20 per cent succumb to eclampsia (a convulsive condition during pregnancy resulting in coma and death). A further 5-10 per cent die of postpartum sepsis and the same number of tetanus. The remaining major causes are bleeding, prolonged labour, and violent deaths.

A law for the protection of women against violence has been on the books since 1960. The Cruelty to Women Act of 1983 enhanced the penalties for offences against women. Although this brought needed public attention to the increasing violence against women, it has had little concrete effect because of a lack of follow-up. UNDP's Human Development Report 1995 states that more than half of all murders of women in Bangladesh are committed by present or former partners.

Especially in times of acute underemployment and economic distress, family conflicts often degenerate into violent acts against women. A study carried out over a period of about ten years documents that rape, physical torture and murder of women are nothing unusual in times of crisis, and that it is precisely women from the lower classes who frequently suffer from anxiety neuroses and depressions. In a society where the perceived honour of the family hinges on the virtue of its female members, rape has especially tragic social consequences for the victim : the shame falls not on the ravisher but upon the ravished.

**Education**

The average educational level of women in Bangladesh is lower than that of men, which is itself shaky enough in comparison with other poor countries. The same applies to primary schooling. In number of school years completed, females lag far behind males especially in rural areas.

Many factors have an influence on women's educational opportunities. Most studies point to poverty as the principal reason why families either fail to enroll their girls in school or withdraw them prematurely from primary school. It is not just that the direct and indirect costs of school attendance are beyond their means, but also that the children are needed at home to perform duties that fall preponderantly on the girls. Extra income plays only a secondary role in the widespread labour demand for girls, since most of them have to work as unpaid labour : in 1990, 3.4 per cent of the girls in the age group ten to fourteen were reported as "economically active" (UNDP, 1995).

Prevailing cultural values and norms appear to have far more significance in the low state of female education, however. Many parents in rural areas lack interest or are openly hostile to the formal education of their daughters for reasons related to social and religious norms in general and to marriage prospects in particular. The opinion is still quite widespread that education spoils a girl's character and undermines her willingness to fulfil her traditional role. Early marriage and the importance of preserving a girl's good reputation lead to widespread withdrawal of girl from school at puberty, especially if they attend coeducational institutions.

Among other factors contributing to gender differentials in enrolments are location and physical facilities of schools, the shortage of female teachers, and a lack of basic amenities (such as latrines). Female education is further constrained by inadequate incentives (food, clothing, and scholarships ) to induce the poor to send girls to school.

**Marriage**

Early marriage, which is a reflection of the low status of women and their low educational attainment, is also a social custom favouring high fertility as well as high maternal mortality. The average age at which girls marry has slightly gone up, though, from 16.4 years in 1970 to 18 years in 1990 (UNDP 1995).

According to the Muslim code of religious law, girls should be wedded at puberty, which can have its onset quite early. An unmarried daughter who is beyond puberty often is still felt to be an embarrassment to the family. Since their economic value is perceived as low, girls are considered a burden on the parental home. Yet at the same time strict norms of behavior keep them from taking up income earning work.

As a rule, the marriage is arranged by the father or another male guardian. Bride and bridegroom do have the right to turn down a match, but it is not customary to make use of this right. Most girls are married to men who are considerably older than themselves. The age difference-averaging seven years at present—confers an additional aura of marital authority on the husbands.

The Dowry Prohibition Act of 1989 forbids the giving and accepting of a dowry under penalty of fine or even prison, but this traditional practice continues nevertheless. If the dowry does not correspond to what the bridegroom or his parents demand, the marriage pact can be broken off, in which case the family of the bride is socially disgraced. As protection against utter destitution should she lose her husband through separation or death, under Islamic law a Bangladeshi woman can lay claim on a certain sum from him, the Mohorana, to be given her either when she marries or in case of divorce. But this does not happen either; first, because many women are not aware of this right and second, because insisting on it would expose a woman to social censure and the risk of losing her husband's goodwill. If a woman does demand the Moharana in case of divorce, then her chances of remarrying plummet. In her husband's family, the wife is subordinate to all the other members of the household—females included. Her only path to social recognition is through motherhood. Male progeny are preferred because, among other reasons, they inherit and it is their duty to provide for the elderly. Owing to the age difference among married couples, women run a high risk of being widowed, with the consequent danger of being left impoverished. In most cases they move out of their parental home without any kind of material cushion that would lend them security and independence. Since under Muslim law women are only inconsequentially entitled to inherit, they must depend on their sons to look after them. This fundamental dependency provides a strong incentive to women to bear as many children as possible and as early as possible as a risk insurance against abrupt poverty.

**Legal Status of Women**

Over and above the constitution in Bangladesh stands the patriarchal interpretation of the law and the religion, which makes implementing egalitarian legislation extremely problematic. Under the constitution, both sexes have the same rights and are entitled to equal treatment under the law. Women also have the right to vote. But a low educational level, illiteracy, a feeble social and political awareness, and the duty to adhere to religious and cultural norms, all act to keep women from taking part in public life.

In family matters such as marriage, divorce, guardianship for children, and rights of inheritance, most people are guided by religious laws, which discriminate quite clearly against women. Under the Islamic law of inheritance, for example, widows receive but a trifling portion of their husband's estate, most particularly if there are no children or "only" daughters. In the absence of a son as male heir, most of the estate passes to the male relatives of the deceased. This law gives women another strong motivation to bear many children. As a rule the wife waives the right to the share (minuscule in any case) due her by law from her husband or parents so as not to jeopardize her chances of assistance in case of acute emergency.

Discrimination against women is further evidenced by the unilateral laws governing polygamy and divorce. Whereas a man can reject his wife without a civil divorce, a woman must go through long drawn-out court proceedings.

The guardianship over children belongs to the husband or to an older male family member. The mother has the duty to care for the sons until they are seven years old, the daughters until puberty. This she is not permitted to do, however, if she marries a second time or, in the judgement of religious doctrine, leads an "immoral" life, i.e., fails to conform to the strictures of *purdah*.

**Purdah— The Seclusion of Women**

The overwhelming majority of women in rural Bangladesh, not only live in grinding poverty but are also exposed to the brunt of the dilemma presented by religious culture and tradition on the one hand and growing poverty as a by-product of landlessness on the other. The behavior that the Muslim faith expects of women is encoded in Purdah—the moral obligation of the woman to live in seclusion, in submission and with modesty. In Bangladesh Purdah is manifested as the strict limitation of women's mobility outside their homestead (*bari*). Women who leave their homestead and enter the public male domain must dress so that body and face are covered. Not to do so would be held a provocative and public offence and would blemish the family's repute. The segregation of the sexes makes the labour market virtually off limits to women. In 1993, the female share of the labour force was a mere 8 per cent (UNDP 1995). Observance of Purdah earns high social and religious prestige, but only the more affluent can afford to stick strictly to the rules.

Men work primarily as agricultural labourers or producers; they are likewise responsible for the selling of agricultural produce and for purchases n the markets. Women, in contrast, are restricted to activities that can be performed within their homestead, as for example, the preparation of foods that are sold in the village or at urban markets as finished products, small livestock keeping, and handicrafts such as spinning, weaving, or needlework. The advantage of such extremely low-paid at-home work is that it collides least with a woman's duties as housewife and mother and with the prescriptions of purdah. The isolation of the woman thus kept busy puts the seal on her powerlessness and ensures male dominance. For reasons of respectability women are not allowed to trade in public. Normally it is the men who bring the product to market and transact business. Often, however, it is also prepubescent girls or post menopausal women, who do not yet or no longer pose a (danger) to society.

With poverty on the increase, however, women are being forced more and more to venture into male domains. The gradual opening of the labour market for them is a two-edged sword, however. Purdah remains so powerful a normative code of proper conduct that manual labour in public brings women appreciable loss of status, exposing them to psychic stress and insecurity. The reputability of the whole family hinges on the invisibility of the woman. Her visible presence in road construction and similar work sectors is a sign of great poverty and desperation—otherwise women would not take on such jobs. The other side of the coin is the opportunity for social change resulting from the emergence of women from their traditional condition of dependence.

The reason for the growing popularity of female labour is not difficult to guess : under the pretence that their weaker physical constitution makes them much less productive they are as a rule paid notably less than men: The average wage for women's non-agricultural labour stands at 42 per cent of the average wage for men (UNDP 1995). The ratio of female wages to male wages is likely to be even lower in rural labour sectors.

**Women's Entitlements in Rural Bangladesh**

Under the rigid rules defining the place and role of the sexes in rural Bangladesh, women are fettered by the contradictions of their purdah-dictated status, which sharply curtails their entitlement to productive resources and even their own labour, while the men's obligation to protect and support the women is governed by normative control. So whereas women's traditional duties continue to be valid unchanged, their normative entitlements are being worn away by advancing relativism, a process that spreading poverty makes particularly acute. It is no surprise that in a social environment such as this, women have scant chance of surviving in a way befitting human dignity.

The relative validity of normative entitlements means

that, with respect to nutrition and health, the intra-household allocation of resources by no means corresponds to the members' needs. Rather it is determined by the individual's place in the family hierarchy, which depends in turn on age, sex and relationship to the household head. This traditional asymmetry in satisfying basic needs translates under condition of absolute poverty into a higher incidence of illness and mortality among women and girls. Women's institutionally limited access to resources and their excessively high dependence on normatively codified entitlements produce specifically gender-linked differences in the process of impoverishment. In 1979 Mead Cain depicted an example of what happens—an example more pertinent than ever today to the lot of rural women:

"One of the women in our sample was the second wife of a relatively rich man. She had been married previously and had a number of children by her former husband. But the time she married for the second time, two of her children had died and one daughter was already married. Her only living son joined her in her new husband's household. The rich husband also had children by his first wife, all of whom had grown up and established their own households by the time of his second marriage.

When, several years after the second marriage, the man died, all his land passed to the children of his first wife. Because the second wife bore him no children, neither she nor her son had any claim to his property upon his death. For various reasons, the widow was unable to turn to the family of her first husband for help. Consequently, she was left with no means of support for herself or her son. She survived by begging, travelling daily to Mymensingh Town (over eight kilometres away) for this purpose. She was permitted to maintain a hut in her deceased husband' *bari*, and she continues to live there with her son. Next to her hut lives one of her stepsons and his family who, aside from occasional handouts, offer her no support. Ironically, the *bari* of her deceased second husband is perhaps the richest per capita in the village, and her brother-in-law, who lives in the same *bari*, is by far the richest man in the village. None of this, however has done the widow any good."

The story shows how dependent the economic status is on that of their husband's and how abruptly they can be plunged into destitution. Because of the striking age differences among married couples, early widowhood before the sons of a union reach employable age is a widespread occurrence.

The increasing number of households headed by women is a further indication of how normative entitlements are eroding, More and more men from the poor strata no longer earn enough to provide for their families. Many leave home for a time or even for good to seek work in the cities. "Seasonal" divorces are the result, particularly in periods of acute food scarcity.

For women, then, the impoverishment process proceeds along several tracks. They become poorer along with the rest of the family, and through the breakdown of the household and the attendant loss of their normative entitlements.

**Women's Status in Bangladesh**

Historically, Bangladesh is a country that has experienced much hardship. Starting in the 18th century, Bangladesh had been considered as a region of British India. By 1947, the country became a province of Pakistan, located hundreds of miles away. Despite this, Bangladesh, then East Pakistan, held a large representation in the Pakistani assembly. In 1970, East Pakistan's Awami League won the Pakistan majority, and by early 1971, the league asserted Bangladesh's independence. Until December of that year, Bangladesh engaged in a civil war with Pakistan that resulted in the loss of a million individuals. With India's aid, Bangladesh defeated Pakistan, and thus, were faced with the business of creating a political structure for the country. This structure proved to be unsteady, as several military coups changed Bangladesh's leadership throughout the 70's and 80's. In 1991, free elections were instituted. But many claimed that the government elections were fraudulent, again creating unrest. During the 1990s, Bangladesh's government was the target of many protests and strikes. The ultimate goal of these actions was to create an environment where new elections could be held. Compounding Bangladesh's problems, too, is the high frequency of natural disasters experienced—like cyclones and floods—the country experienced in the years following independence. It's people have been plagued by famine. Factoring in all these conditions, it is evident that Bangladesh is a country whose people face severe economic plight.

# 4

# Discrimination Against Women

Violence Against Women (VAW), particularly by husbands is common in Bangladesh. The nature of violence ranges from scolding to severe beating, forced sex and in extreme cases murder. Gender inequality, economic dependence of women on their husband and patriarchal system reinforce each other to perpetuate and promote VAW. Unreasonable sexual demand by husbands, suspicion of extra marital relationship by either partners, perceived neglect of husband by wife and continued demand for dowry are dominant reasons for the conflict leading to different forms of VAW. The patriarchal system and prevailing gender inequality have conditioned women's mentality to the extent that many women justified husband's beating and forced sex as their right. What hurt them most is insult in presence of others than beating by husbands behind the closed door.

Working women at the initial stage of their life had faced more violence than non working, perhaps because they challenged established gender role. Violence against women divided into four parts.

- The social context of gender violence in Bangladesh;
- The scale and social dimensions of particular forms of violence;
- A brief analysis is provided of the legal mechanisms designed to protect women, and their operation;
- Some details of the actions of women is organisations against violence, with suggestions for further contacts, are provided.

Jahan says the ambiguity surrounding the question of violence against women in Bangladeshi society. On the one hand, violence is held in repugnancei and may provoke outrage. For example, a man who sprayed acid on and killed his new wife, on grounds of her inadequate dowry, was hacked to death by villagers in Northern Bangladesh. On the other hand, violence against women is accepted, tolerated and in certain prescribed forms and given contexts it is legitimated. Jahan relates this to the fact that gender inequality, leading to gender violence, is deeply embedded in the Bangladeshi social structure; all Bangladeshi social institutions permit, even encourage the demonstration of unequal power relations between the sexesi.

The legitimation of male violence, especially battering, allows it to be seen (by women as well as men), as a deserved response to female transgression of male demands or controls. Thus, women feel shame and guilt - as well as anger in some cases - which militates against the reporting of battering. Murder, acid throwing and abduction may suffer less from stigma in reporting.

Other factors contributing to the under-reporting of violence against women include: the lack of awareness among women of their legal rights; the perception that their cases will be treated with derision and/or ignored by the police; and the fear that making charges will compound problems with their husband and his kin. Rape probably evokes the greatest feelings of shame among women, and thus is most likely to be under-reported. Nevertheless, Jahan suggests that the rise in reported crime against women in Bangladesh may reflect a rise in the reporting of rape, but also an increase in the incidence of assaults on women and in the proportion of female victims of violent crimes. She notes that in 1980, 12.4 percent of the victims of all reported violent crime were female, whereas by 1984, the Few studies of the scale and nature of violence against women in Bangladesh have been carried out, and therefore much of this section is based on an analysis of three studies discussed in Jahan. These are: Akanda and Shamin is study of violence leading to murder; the analysis by UBINIG (Unnayan Bihalper Niti Nirdhaoni Gobeshona - Policy Research for Development Alternatives) of the coverage of rape in two daily newspapers, from 1981 to 1984; and Islam and Begumis study of male violence reported in one newspaper in 1975-84.

Jahan also presents evidence from Women for Women, a Dhaka-based research and study group, who have sponsored a research project on violence against women. This evidence is supported by other studies of rural Bangladesh which discuss wife-beating and/or rape, i.e: Hartmann and Boyce; Kabeer; White. The formal studies analyse only violence against women, while recognising that its occurrence is much more widespread than the reported figures would suggest.

Kondkher and Jahan also say arise in the availability of weapons such as guns and acid, and also the increased portrayal of violence in the mass media in imported films, as factors which may be associated with the rise in violent crimes, including those against women. The Scale and Social Dimensions of Crimes Against Women Battering of women. The battering of women within the household appears to be widespread throughout Bangladesh. Roy notes from a study carried out by the Bangladesh Rural Advancement Committee (BRAC) in Jamal pur, that most women who are beaten suffer from beatings every week which are severe enough to leave marks on the body and cause pain for several daysí. Such beatings may be related to dowry, to the perceived failure of a woman, particularly a wife, to fulfil her household duties, or to be ëproperlyí humble and obedient; or they may serve as an outlet for male frustration. Numerous commentators have remarked on beating as a ëpunishmentí for failing to do the husband is bidding.

Akanda and Shamin cite the case of Roushan Ara in Rangpur who was beaten to death for failing to stitch twc buttons onto her husband is shirt; Gardener describes women in Sylhet being beaten for infractions such as the evening meal not being ready on time, or tasting it whilst cooking. Hartmann and Boyce cite the case of a woman whose husband beat herë because thechickens stole a few grains of riceí, in a village in Rajshahi Division, North-West Bangladesh. Men beating women is further compounded by the absolute poverty and powerlessness of most of the rural population of Bangladesh. Kabeer suggests that many men vent their own frustration at their poverty and inability to fulfil their role as the male provider, according to gender based norms, by battering their wives. In the words of one of the Katni villagers in Hartmann and Boyceís study, ë When my husband is stomach is empty, he beats me, but when it is full, there is peaceí. Kabeer says the seasonality of such beatings -they increased during kartik, the hungry season in August-October, and before the main harvest in November-December.

None of these studies explicitly discuss whether children are subject to similar violence, and if so, whether the extent and severity of such beatings differs by gender. White, studying a village in Faridpur district, notes that the escalation of dowry demands over the last 40 years has created another manifestation of violence against women. Dowry demands among Muslims and Christians in Bangladesh are a relatively new phenomenon and while the scale of demands may not have reached that of urban India, White notes a tendency for men to explicitly claim that the inadequate dowry they have received gives them a3 Light beating of a wife by a husband is sanctioned in the Quran, though Sisters in Islam point out that this is a codification of early Arabian custom and is permissive rather than mandatory. If a wife still refuses to do the husband is bidding, he should not strike her again. Sisters in Islam are a Malaysian women is organisation, formed in 1988, who are engaged in conciousness raising and educational work on issues relating to the status of women in Islam and Muslim family laws. Their booklet, Are Muslim Men Allowed to Beat Their Wives?, was published in 1991, in response to attempts in certain quarters of the political establishment to dilute or veto new legislation on Domestic violence, on the grounds that it should not contradict Muslim teachings.

**Murder of Women**

In the words of one man, take out the difference in beatingí. While a certain level of beating may be tolerated and accepted as one of the gender dimensions of the social order in Bangladesh, severe brutality may provoke community outrage. Hartmann and Boyce says a case of angry villagers tying up and assaulting a man who had beaten his wife too brutally. White mentions that in Faridpur district, a bichar (a community hearing) might take place, in such cases. It is rare that the battering of women within the household is reported to the police. However, recently a judge in Rangpur has been fined 5,000 taka ($125) for wife-beating. The murder of women by their husbands and in-laws is associated with both the escalation of dowry demands, and with the more general harassment and severe beating of women. It is possible that, as in India, women are murdered if their dowries are too small; if the woman is disliked by her husband or his kin; if her household skills are perceived to be lacking; or even if her skin is too dark. Often such murders are arranged to look like accidents, or suicides, with bodies being suspended to resemble a hanging, insecticides being poured down the dead woman is throat or burning being passed off as a cooking accident. Like beating, the murder of women appears to be carried out by husbands and in-laws, in distinction to sexual violence, which is more often carried out, or at least reported to have been carried out, by unknown men. However, various reports suggest an increase in fatal mugging, acid-throwing and other attacks by outsiders. Jahan and Hartmann and Boyce suggest that many women are in fact driven to suicide by constant beating, harassment and the feeling that there is no escape.

**Acid-throwing and Mugging**

There is little firm evidence on these forms of violence against women. Reports to the police of acid-throwing remain few in number - there were 27 such attacks on women recorded in 1985. It has been suggested that women is increased presence in the public sphere, transgressing the traditional boundaries of purdah, is a source of outrage among some men and may therefore be leading to an increase of attacks of this kind on women. Abduction Khondker cites 519 reported abductions of women or girls in Bangladesh in 1985, and 509 in 1986. While some of these women and girls may be forced into prostitution, Khan and Are feen show that this is fairly uncommon.

**Rape of Minor Girls**

The 35 percent of reported rapes involve minor girls, i.e. those under 15. The social ostracization of raped women is much noted - women are widely believed to be responsible for their own rape, perhaps due to prevailing ideas about women is powerful sexuality, and men is inability to control themselves. In law, it is considered that for a husband to force sexual intercourse on his wife constitutes rape in Bangladesh Legal Provisions on Violence Against Women.

There are two main laws relating to violence against women in Bangladesh: The Cruelty to Women Ordinance and

The Dowry Prohibition Act. There are also articles in the Penal Code relating to rape. The Cruelty to Women Ordinance outlaws the kidnapping and abduction of women and acid throwing attacks on women, and mandates the death penalty or life imprisonment for causing the death of a rape victim. The same provisions apply to a husband and his family under the Dowry Prohibition Act, for the murder or attempted murder of a woman for dowry. Article 376 of the Penal Code mandates two years imprisonment, a fine, or both, for the rape of a woman by her husband. Article 342, however, requires that a woman undergo a medical examination immediately after rape, which in practice, minimizes the possibility of a conviction being made. In any legal case, including cases of violence against women, if the complainant is absent, the case can be dismissed. In practise this discriminates against women who may be intimidated by their husbands or in-laws into staying away from court. In practice, convictions for rape and other violent crimes against women are rarely made, because women are unaware of their legal rights, because legal institutions are male-dominated and often inaccessible or unsympathetic to women, because of the difficulties of proving the case, because of legal lóopholes, and because of an underlying undervaluation of women. Response of Women is Organisations in Bangladesh to Violence Against Women The main strategies employed by women is organisations in Bangladesh, to combat violence against women, have been: publicizing and organising around particular cases; legal awareness work; and conscientization of both women and men on issues of gender violence. Nari Pokkho, a small autonomous women's group, and Bangladesh Mahila Parishad, have both always been vocal on issues of gender-based violence. Bangladesh Mahila Parishad, formally linked to the Communist party ,provides legal assistance to women, has organised demonstrations around dowry cases, and has set up some battered women is shelters. Kabeer suggests that Mahila Parishad is links with the Communist Party may prevent it giving independent significance to women is oppression. The Government of Bangladesh and Women's Affairs Directorate have also established some hostels for battered and threatened women, and offers counselling services. However, Jahan questions the relevance of battered women is shelters in the Bangladeshi context, when for most women, both psychologically and materially, leaving the ësecurityí of their marital home is impossible. She calls rather for greater community mobilisation around gender violence, whilst recognising that this may be difficult to achieve. Bangladesh Jatiyo Mahila Ainjibi Samity - the National Association of Women Lawyers - has organised legal awareness classes aiming to reach 50 million women.

**Legal Issues**

One of the primary foci of Ain-o-Shalish Kendro, a women-oriented legal issues and aid group formed in 1989, is domestic violence (Anne Marie Goetz, personal communication). Bangladesh Rural Advancement Committee (BRAC), a large rural development NGO, whose grassroots membership consists of 70 percent women, has decided to set up women is legal aid centres in all its area development offices. This arises from a recent study carried out for BRAC on domestic violence, which has not yet been translated into English, but which documents the severity of marital violence faced by women. Grassroots NGOs such as Nijera Kori, Saptagram and Proshika are active inconscientizing women and men on issues of violence, and Grameen Bank organisers may also be working in this area.

**Prostitution**

One study on prostitution in Bangladesh is available. This focuses on prostitution in Natinagar, one of the four red light districts of Dhaka, and in Ananda bazar, one of the three such districts in Narayanganj. It is estimated that there are approximately 2000 prostitutes in each of these two areas. The main types of prostitution are: in brothels, where women are organised under sardanis (madams); street-walking; in hotels, especially in Dhaka; and in rented houses. In addition, baijis (dancing girls), and escorts, who may or may not engage in sexual intercourse, a reactive in these districts.

Khan and Are feen found that, contrary to popular opinion, the majority of prostitutes were not abducted and had chosen the profession, perceiving it to have major economic advantages and also feeling that they had no alternative skills with which to secure a livelihood. Generally, the prostitutes in the study were well-nourished but many suffered from untreated sexually transmitted diseases. Rates of contraceptive usage were relativelyhigh, but only a small percentage of women used condoms, thus increasing their exposure to HIV infection. Prostitution without a licence is illegal and carries a sentence of two years imprisonment or a fine, although in practice seven days is the normal sentence. Prostitutes are vulnerable to exploitation by pimps or sardanis and by muscle-men (mantans) who organise protection.

The general state and societal perception of prostitutes is of socially deviant women, who need to be rehabilitated into society. The rehabilitation of prostitutes through corrective institutions is seen as necessary. Such institutionsë place such women in the protective custody of the state until they have been taught how to conform more closely to the social norms of poor but virtuous womanhood. IWRAW and Kabeer, such institutions are much disliked by prostitutes because of the infringement of their rights to go out or see relatives and friends. Shamin says that prostitution is not confined tourban areas, but forms one of a range of survival strategies of some poor rural women. For urban prostitutes, by contrast, prostitution tends to constitute their sole means of livelihood. BRAC may be collaborating with Ain-o-Shalish Kendro to develop these centres, but this is unconfirmed.

# 5

# Women's Participation in Government

The globalization of the world's economy and the deepening interdependence among nations present challenges and opportunities for sustained economic growth and development, as well as risks and uncertainties for the future of the world economy. The uncertain global economic climate has been accompanied by economic restructuring as well as, in a certain number of countries, persistent, unmanageable levels of external debt and structural adjustment programmes. In addition, all types of conflict, displacement of people and environmental degradation have undermined the capacity of Governments to meet the basic needs of their populations. Transformations in the world economy are profoundly changing the parameters of social development in all countries. One significant trend has been the increased poverty of women, the extent of which varies from region to region. Migration and consequent changes in family structures have placed additional burdens on women, especially those who provide for several dependants. Macroeconomic policies need rethinking and reformulation to address such trends. These policies focus almost exclusively on the formal sector. They also tend to impede the initiatives of women and fail to consider the differential impact on women and men. The application of gender analysis to a wide range of policies and programmes is therefore critical to poverty reduction strategies. In order to eradicate poverty and achieve sustainable development, women and men must participate fully and equally in the formulation of macroeconomic and social policies and strategies for the eradication of poverty. The eradication of poverty cannot be accomplished through anti-poverty programmes alone but will require democratic participation and changes in economic structures in order to ensure access for all women to resources, opportunities and public services.

**Women's Poverty**

Poverty may be caused by an economic recession that results in loss of livelihood or by disaster or conflict. There is also the poverty of low-wage workers and the utter destitution of people who fall outside family support systems, social institutions and safety nets. In the past decade the number of women living in poverty has increased disproportionately to the number of men, particularly in the developing countries.

The feminization of poverty has also recently become a significant problem in the countries with economies in transition as a short-term consequence of the process of political, economic and social transformation. In addition to economic factors, the rigidity of socially ascribed gender roles and women's limited access to power, education, training and productive resources as well as other emerging factors that may lead to insecurity for families are also responsible. The failure to adequately mainstream a gender perspective in all economic analysis and planning and to address the structural causes of poverty is also a contributing factor. Women contribute to the economy and to combating poverty through both remunerated and unremunerated work at home, in the community and in the workplace. The empowerment of women is a critical factor in the eradication of poverty. While poverty affects households as a whole, because of the gender division of labour and responsibilities for household welfare, women bear a disproportionate burden, attempting to manage household consumption and production under conditions of increasing scarcity. Poverty is particularly acute for women living in rural households.

Women's poverty is directly related to the absence of economic opportunities and autonomy, lack of access to economic resources, including credit, land ownership and inheritance, lack of access to education and support services and their minimal participation in the decision-making process.

Poverty can also force women into situations in which they are vulnerable to sexual exploitation. In too many countries, social welfare systems do not take sufficient account of the specific conditions of women living in poverty, and there is a tendency to scale back the services provided by such systems. The risk of falling into poverty is greater for women than for men, particularly in old age, where social security systems are based on the principle of continuous remunerated employment. In some cases, women do not fulfil this requirement because of interruptions in their work, due to the unbalanced distribution of remunerated and unremunerated work. Moreover, older women also face greater obstacles to labour-market re-entry. In many developed countries, where the level of general education and professional training of women and men are similar and where systems of protection against discrimination are available, in some sectors the economic transformations of the past decade have strongly increased either the unemployment of women or the precarious nature of their employment.

The release of women's productive potential is pivotal to breaking the cycle of poverty so that women can share fully in the benefits of development and in the products of their own labour. Sustainable development and economic growth that is both sustained and sustainable are possible only through improving the economic, social, political, legal and cultural status of women.

**Social Development**

Equitable social development that recognizes empowering the poor, particularly women, to utilize environmental resources sustainably is a necessary foundation for sustainable development. The success of policies and measures aimed at supporting or strengthening the promotion of gender equality and the improvement of the status of women should be based on the integration of the gender perspective in general policies relating to all spheres of society as well as the implementation of positive measures with adequate institutional and financial support at all levels. The Governments should take the following actions to review, adopt and maintain macroeconomic policies and development strategies that address the needs and efforts of women in poverty:

- Analyse, from a gender perspective, policies and programmes - including those related to macroeconomic stability, structural adjustment, external debt problems, taxation, investments, employment, markets and all relevant sectors of the economy - with respect to their impact on poverty, on inequality and particularly on women; assess their impact on family well-being and conditions and adjust them, as appropriate, to promote more equitable distribution of productive assets, wealth, opportunities, income and services;
- Pursue and implement sound and stable macroeconomic and sectoral policies that are designed and monitored with the full and equal participation of women, encourage broad-based sustained economic growth, address the structural causes of poverty and are geared towards eradicating poverty and reducing gender-based inequality within the overall framework of achieving people-centred sustainable development;
- Restructure and target the allocation of public expenditures to promote women's economic opportunities and equal access to productive resources and to address the basic social, educational and health needs of women, particularly those living in poverty;
- Develop agricultural and fishing sectors, where and as necessary, in order to ensure, as appropriate, household and national food security and food self-sufficiency, by allocating the necessary financial, technical and human resources;
- Develop policies and programmes to promote equitable distribution of food within the household;
- Provide adequate safety nets and strengthen State-based and community-based support systems, as an integral part of social policy, in order to enable women living in poverty to withstand adverse economic environments and preserve their livelihood, assets and revenues in times of crisis;
- Generate economic policies that have a positive impact on the employment and income of women workers in both the formal and informal sectors and adopt specific measures to address women's unemployment, in particular their long-term unemployment;

- Formulate and implement, when necessary, specific economic, social, agricultural and related policies in support of female-headed households;
- Develop and implement anti-poverty programmes, including employment schemes, that improve access to food for women living in poverty, including through the use of appropriate pricing and distribution mechanisms;
- Ensure the full realization of the human rights of all women migrants, including women migrant workers, and their protection against violence and exploitation; introduce measures for the empowerment of documented women migrants, including women migrant workers; facilitate the productive employment of documented migrant women through greater recognition of their skills, foreign education and credentials, and facilitate their full integration into the labour force;
- Introduce measures to integrate or reintegrate women living in poverty and socially marginalized women into productive employment and the economic mainstream; ensure that internally displaced women have full access to economic opportunities and that the qualifications and skills of immigrant and refugee women are recognized;
- Enable women to obtain affordable housing and access to land by, among other things, removing all obstacles to access, with special emphasis on meeting the needs of women, especially those living in poverty and female heads of household;
- Formulate and implement policies and programmes that enhance the access of women agricultural and fisheries producers (including subsistence farmers and producers, especially in rural areas) to financial, technical, extension and marketing services; provide access to and control of land, appropriate infrastructure and technology in order to increase women's incomes and promote household food security, especially in rural areas and, where appropriate, encourage the development of producer-owned, market-based cooperatives;
- Create social security systems wherever they do not exist, or review them with a view to placing individual women and men on an equal footing, at every stage of their lives;

- Ensure access to tree or low-cost legal services, including legal literacy, especially designed to reach women living in poverty;
- Take particular measures to promote and strengthen policies and programmes for indigenous women with their full participation and respect for their cultural diversity, so that they have opportunities and the possibility of choice in the development process in order to eradicate the poverty that affects them;
- In accordance with the commitments made at the World Summit for Social Development, seek to mobilize new and additional financial resources that are both adequate and predictable and mobilized in a way that maximizes the availability of such resources and uses all available funding sources and mechanisms with a view to contributing towards the goal of poverty eradication and targeting women living in poverty;
- Strengthen analytical capacity in order to more systematically strengthen gender perspectives and integrate them into the design and implementation of lending programmes, including structural adjustment and economic recovery programmes;
- Find effective development-oriented and durable solutions to external debt problems in order to help them to finance programmes and projects targeted at development, including the advancement of women, inter alia, through the immediate implementation of the terms of debt forgiveness agreed upon in the Paris Club in December 1994, which encompassed debt reduction, including cancellation or other debt relief measures and develop techniques of debt conversion applied to social development programmes and projects in conformity with the priorities of the Platform for Action;
- Invite the international financial institutions to examine innovative approaches to assisting low-income countries with a high proportion of multilateral debt, with a view to alleviating their debt burden;
- Ensure that structural adjustment programmes are designed to minimize their negative effects on vulnerable and disadvantaged groups and communities and to

- Encourage links between financial institutions and non-governmental organizations and support innovative lending practices, including those that integrate credit with women's services and training and provide credit facilities to rural women.

Commercial banks, financial institutions and the private sector should take the following actions:

- Use credit and savings methodologies that are effective in reaching women in poverty and innovative in reducing transaction costs and redefining risk;
- Open special windows for lending to women, including young women, who lack access to traditional sources of collateral;
- Simplify banking practices, for example by reducing the minimum deposit and other requirements for opening bank accounts;
- Ensure the participation and joint ownership, where possible, of women clients in the decision-making of institutions providing credit and financial services.

Multilateral and bilateral development cooperation organizations should take the following actions:

- Support, through the provision of capital and/or resources, financial institutions that serve low-income, small-scale and micro-scale women entrepreneurs and producers, in both the formal and informal sectors.
- Support institutions that meet performance standards in reaching large numbers of low-income women and men through capitalization, refinancing and institutional development support in forms that foster self-sufficiency.
- Increase funding for programmes and projects designed to promote sustainable and productive entrepreneurial activities for income- generation among disadvantaged women and women living in poverty.

The Governments should taken the following actions to develop gender-based methodologies and conduct research to address the feminization of poverty:

- Develop conceptual and practical methodologies for incorporating gender perspectives into all aspects of economic policy-making, including structural adjustment planning and programmes;

- Apply these methodologies in conducting gender-impact analyses of all policies and programmes, including structural adjustment programmes, and disseminate the research findings;
- Collect gender and age-disaggregated data on poverty and all aspects of economic activity and develop qualitative and quantitative statistical indicators to facilitate the assessment of economic performance from a gender perspective.

The United Nations Development Programme has estimated that 1.3 billion people in the developing world are poor. Women represent approximately 70 percent of this figure, yet, as a group, they work longer hours relative to men and contribute more in terms of social reproduction. The causes of poverty are complex and go beyond economics; political, cultural, social and religious institutions and processes are implicated in the production and perpetuation of poverty.

We discuss the conceptual frameworks through which poverty is often analysed, and emphasise the need to incorporate more complete considerations and interpretations of women's and men's lived experiences. Within this context, we examine ways in which traditional conceptualisations and interpretations erase and obscure gendered dimensions of poverty and most often result in the formulation and implementation of policies that fail to improve the lives of poor women and their families. We conclude with several practical policy recommendations for identifying and redressing poverty in general and its gendered dimensions in particular

**Poverty From a Gender Perspective**

The experience of poverty is both shared and distributed within families. All suffer but some suffer more than others. Poverty is tied to a lack of access to productive resources, physical goods and income which results in individual and/or group deprivation, vulnerability and powerlessness. It has various manifestations including hunger and malnutrition, ill-health, and limited or no access to education, health care, and safe housing and (paid) work environments. It also includes experiences of economic, political and social discrimination.

Within this context, poverty must be viewed both in its *absolute* and *relative* dimensions. Although very useful, government-defined poverty lines refer only to absolute poverty. Relative poverty refers to the individual's or group's position in the social scale, that is, to a low position in the hierarchies of class and other inequalities, a dimension not captured by absolute poverty lines. For example, within the same household, women and female children may be relatively poorer than other household members or they may be deprived of basic needs even if the household itself does not fall within the defined absolute poverty line. In this sense, the presence of poverty is inseparably linked to inequality in the distribution of resources and income.

**Transient Poverty**

Distinctions between *structural* or chronic and *transient* poverty are particularly useful for understanding the lived experiences of poor women. Structural poverty is rooted in socio-economic and political institutions, is experienced over the long term, and is often transferred intergenerationally. Rural populations with little or no access to land and other productive resources, with living standards below the poverty line, and/or with chronic under-employment or unemployment exemplify this type of poverty. Gendered dimensions of structural poverty are based, in many instances, on the institutional - specifically legal and cultural - denial of land and other productive resources, including vocational and educational training, to women. In contrast, transient poverty is due to cyclical or temporary factors and is experienced over shorter periods of time, such as with cyclical unemployment, inflation, macro-economic policy shifts, and/or natural disasters. Within the current global economy, technological changes often lead to transient poverty among women with low education and skill levels. It is important to note that the presence of one form of poverty in a region or country does not preclude the presence of another. Poverty - transient and structural - can also be policy-induced.

During the last fifteen years, the implementation of structural adjustment programmes (SAPs) in many low-income countries have provided examples of policy-induced poverty. Numerous studies have shown that the combination of economic restructuring, government budget cuts, inflation, privatisation, shifts in resource allocation, and unemployment have generated deep social costs and led to the feminisation and urbanisation of poverty.

Thus, despite an ever-increasing productive capacity of the world economy, there is a reversal of previous trends of decreasing poverty levels in many countries. The social costs of adjustment have raised many questions about, and criticisms of, economic models that led to the orthodox and hegemonic adjustment packages of the 1980s and 1990s. Critiques of adjustment emphasising the effects on the poor have come from a variety of sources. In addition, studies have illustrated gender dimensions of adjustment, effectively disputing the belief that macroeconomic policies are gender and class neutral. Large cuts in social service programmes such as health care, child care, family planning and education, and increases in the prices of basic goods and services have severely affected poor and middle-class households. Women and girls often carry the heaviest burden of economic adjustment because of their reproductive roles and/or household divisions of labour. Adjustment packages have intensified their workload by increasing their participation in formal and informal labour markets.

Women often assume the responsibility for "making ends meet" when real incomes fall. This is accomplished through what has been called "packaging", a term referring to the performance of several jobs in either or both the formal and informal economic sectors, typically resulting in an intensification of women's workloads. Similarly, studies on the effects of adjustment on agricultural communities have documented ways in which gender relations mediate the dynamics of adjustment. Thus, structural adjustment has illustrated how macroeconomic policies that work through and within gendered structures and relations shape the choices and material conditions of women and men differently.

Within the current global economy, poverty is being generated through other processes as well. Widespread economic restructuring has led to rapid increased levels of unemployment reaching crisis proportions in many countries, increased flexibilisation and insecurity in labour markets, informalisation, technological changes, the downsizing of the industrial workforce, and income polarisation. These processes can be observed in both high- and low-income countries. They have resulted in social polarisations and increased poverty for those who become unemployed and lack the necessary skills required by current labour markets. Thus poverty is linked to the inability of the economic system to generate a sufficient number of jobs to absorb the unemployed and the underemployed. Again, these processes have specific gender dimensions, including higher levels of female vis-ý-vis male unemployment, informalisation of work often performed by women, and increased participation of women in the precarious informal sector.

**Poverty and Education**

The precarious position of poor women in the global economy is in part related to low educational levels, including high levels of illiteracy, in many countries. According to the Human Development Report, in 1990 the illiteracy rate among women was approximately 19 percent in South East Asia and 17 percent in Latin America. High illiteracy rates are still prevalent in North and sub-Saharan Africa and South Asia. In countries with high illiteracy rates, "the illiteracy rate among women aged 15-24 is at least 25 percentage points higher than among young men". During the last 20 years, combined female enrollment in primary and secondary schools increased across regions, but a significant proportion of the female population continues to have little or no access to educational institutions. For example, though the countries in the Middle East and North Africa almost doubled female enrollment in elementary and secondary schools from 32 percent in 1970 to 60 percent in 1992, approximately 40 percent of the female population continues to be uneducated.

Similarly, sub-Saharan Africa has an enrollment rate of 49 percent and South Asia 55 percent. Overall illiteracy rates have decreased among adults in low-income countries but the percentage of illiterate women in the world is higher than the percentage of illiterate men. Additionally, illiteracy rates for young women in rural communities are consistently two to three times higher than those of women in urban areas. Family preferences to educate boys, and the need for subsistence agricultural labour, are often cited as factors limiting the education of girls in rural communities. This point underlines the necessity for situation specific analysis in order to formulate successful poverty eradication policies.

**The Distribution of Work**

Another dimension of women's well-being (or lack thereof) is related to the unequal distribution of work and leisure according to gender. Women work longer hours than men in most countries of the world and often carry a disproportionate share of the burden of coping with poverty. This is clearly seen in studies regarding women's and men's use of time. A comparison of time use for women and men in rural and urban communities reveals that women spend an average of 20 percent more time relative to men working in rural areas and six percent more in urban areas. This difference is often a result of women's reproductive roles, their greater responsibility for agricultural work in family-owned farms, and barriers to their entry in urban labour markets. A review of 31 countries indicates that:

- of the total work performed, women work an average of 55 percent more than men in low-income countries and 51 percent in high-income countries;
- of men's total work time in high-income countries, approximately 67 percent is spent in paid activities and one third in unpaid activities. For women, these statistics are reversed.

In low-income countries, more than 75 percent of women's work is in unpaid activities. Given that the system of national accounts (SNA), was designed to measure income and output -as produced, exchanged, and measured through the market - rather than human well-being, much of the non-market work performed in all societies remains statistically invisible. As a result, those who perform unpaid tasks are not economically rewarded, nor socially valued or recognized as productive members of society.

Time use studies also indicate that women adjust their work patterns to accommodate their specific economic environments and family needs. According to Agarwal "women's work", particularly work performed by poor women, is strongly affected by environmental degradation. For example, deforestation and overgrazing of pasture land often causes soil erosion which result in decreases in the supply of fuel wood and depletion of water resources. These changes result in increases in the time and energy that is used to collect water and wood for fuel. Therefore, when land and water is depleted, much more labour (disproportionately women's labour) is required to maintain the same level of production. Additionally, the workload of girls increases relative to boys, which in turn negatively affects the educational levels of girls. Gendered dimensions of poverty can be understood by using the notions of *entitlement* and *capabilities* to discuss poverty and gender biases as well as policies to address them. Amartya Sen has defined entitlements as the "bundle of goods over which [people] can establish ownership through production and trade, using their own means". Capabilities, on the other hand, have been defined as the alternative combination of "functionings" - or "doings and beings" a person achieves - from which a person can choose. These benchmarks are useful for the evaluation of factors related to the gendered dimensions of poverty. For example, poor women's relatively low entitlements are at the source of their dependency, vulnerability, and low degree of autonomy. Similarly, their limited capabilities, such as in cases of illiteracy or low educational levels, tend to lock them in the vicious circle of poverty and deprivation.

An analysis of entitlements and capabilities provides an essential starting point for gender-sensitive poverty eradication strategies. Such an analysis highlights the importance of focusing on women's entitlements, through increasing their access to land ownership and use, credit, and other productive resources that have the potential to facilitate income generation. Likewise, such an analysis emphasises the gendered (that is, socially determined) nature not only of women's and men's differential capabilities but, significantly, their ability to develop and deploy these capabilities in order to move out of poverty. An understanding of the ways in which entitlements and capabilities are socially, and not merely individually, determined is illuminated by the notions of *preferences* and *rights*. Diane Elson has enriched analyses of poverty and gender bias in development through her exploration of preferences and rights as contrasting frames of reference within which analysis may be undertaken. She states that placing emphasis on preferences as opposed to rights or vice versa affects our evaluation of the factors affecting poverty and leads to different policy implications. For example, neoclassical economic analyses tend to emphasise that women's and men's entitlements, their location within the economy and, by implication, their experiences with poverty, are largely the result of their preferences and choices. In this view, poverty among women is linked to their choices regarding work - both within the household and in the paid labour market - and to their reproductive choices. This type of argument fails to take into consideration the institutional barriers and obstacles to exercising choices and the many possible limits set by initial entitlements. Women's poor entitlements and their limited mobility relative to men in most countries often affect their preferences and limit their choices.

While emphasis has been placed on women's rights during the past two decades, much remains to be done in terms of dismantling gender bias and ensuring the successful implementation of laws regarding women's rights, including economic rights. Additionally, a focus on rights, as Elson has pointed out, has to be supplemented by an emphasis on the socially conferred and constrained nature of women's capabilities, understood as what women are able to do. Gender discrimination in the labour market and the social stigma sometimes attached to women's participation in paid production, coupled with expectations that their reproductive role calls for a primary concentration on household work, are examples of constraints that define women's capabilities. These concepts can be used not only to best understand the complexity of factors that result in gendered dimensions of poverty, but as a framework for policy in and of itself. Given that the eradication of poverty is a component of human development, defined as "a process of enlarging people's choices" the concepts described above can help shape policy directions to address gender specific dimensions of poverty. This implies a focus on:

— entitlements, such as land and credit policies that increase access to resources for poor women and men;

- increasing capabilities, as with training programmes and access to marketing networks; and
- integrating gender as a category of analysis in international and national debates on poverty and in the formulation of appropriate economic, political, and social policies and programmes/projects to eradicate poverty.

These actions have the potential to increase the possibilities of meeting individual preferences and rights.

**Gender's Development Policy**

Mainstream development theories, policies, and strategies have analysed poverty through what has been described as a gender-blind or gender-neutral lens. However, most approaches are in fact not neutral because they assume the male actor as the standard and representative of the human actor. Consequently, gender-neutral policies address women's lived experiences, needs, interests, and constraints only to the extent to which they conform to or overlap with the norms set by the male actor. Within the context of poverty analyses, this leads to misdiagnoses of poverty processes through the erasure of its gendered dimensions.

Additionally, policies and strategies developed to assist "the poor" have often focused on men's roles or on institutions such as the household or the family, with the assumption that women would benefit as equally as men. One such example is that of social investment funds that have been implemented in many low-income countries to assist "the poor" during the process of structural adjustment. Although some of the projects have been designed to assist women, the most common presupposition has been that women will benefit alongside men from project implementation.

The operationalisation of social investment funds has ignored women and proved unable to address the specific needs of women living in poverty. This is principally because the lived experiences of poor women are rarely conceptualised. When their material realities are theorised, women are primarily perceived in the roles of dependent wives and mothers and they are as a result incorporated into policies only in terms of these family roles. Thus, when projects are implemented specifically for women, they are most often formulated from limited, stereotypical, and essentialist notions of femininity. They consequently reinforce women's subordinate positions within their households and communities, as with microenterprise projects that promote low-paid craft production for women without training them in marketing or other better-paid skills.

Traditional poverty eradication measures also prioritise the provision of "basic" goods and services (such as food, housing, health care, and education) to poor women and men without questioning the role(s) of economic, political, and social institutions and ideologies that are implicated in the production and perpetuation of poverty processes. One such measure is a microenterprise development project in Cali, Colombia. This programme provides training and counseling in business administration and credit to existing microentrepreneurs. There is no economic literacy programme provided to the participants about SAPs or the impact of macroeconomic policy on their lives.

Additionally, these programmes are not likely to get women out of poverty because they do not provide access to productive resources on a permanent basis. It is therefore important to integrate a gender perspective within these programmes, an integration that should take place from the bottom up on the basis of needs and policies identified by women. The social investment funds in Latin America provide an interesting context for such an effort to integrate a gender perspective since they have been operationalised through a process of decentralisation and have often encouraged a shift of initiatives to the community and/or local level. Feminist scholars have provided alternative and more complete ways of analysing development from a gender perspective. Since the appearance of Ester Boserup's book "Women's Role in Economic Development" in 1970, much has been done to highlight the differential impact of development on women. Yet, the persistence and, in some cases intensification, of old problems such as poverty exemplifies the insufficiency of this approach. Policy makers and practitioners must consider both the material realities in which women and men are immersed and the ways in which institutions and ideologies (political, economic, cultural, and religious) position women and men and impact their lives differently. Thus, using Michelle

Barrett's terminology, it is important to analyse "words" as well as "things" to understand the gendered dimensions of development in general and poverty in particular. This implies that our understanding of poverty as it is experienced by women must include factors attached to its *meaning* as well as the material elements with which it is interlinked.

Both factors (the meaning of poverty and its material elements) contribute to the perpetuation of poverty and need to be addressed. As Elson has stated:

> Overcoming male bias is not simply a matter of persuasion, argument, change in viewpoint in everyday attitudes, in theoretical reasoning, and in policy process. It also requires changes in the deep structures of economic and social life, and collective action, not simply individual action.

It is also critical to incorporate in this analysis an understanding of gender relations, understood as relations of power between women and men that partially determine the terms on which they interact. Gender relations are revealed in a range of practices, including the division of labour and resources, and through ideologies and representations, such as the ascribing to women and men different abilities, attitudes, desires, personality traits, and behavioral patterns. Policies that are informed by the analyses above will address gender-specific needs of both poor women and men.

Gender-transformative policy can hope to provide women with the enabling resources which will allow them to take greater control of their own lives, to determine what kinds of gender relations they want to live within, and to devise the strategies and alliances to help them get there.

To be successful, gender-sensitive poverty eradication measures must be specific to the country, region, and locality of the targeted community. The formulation of context-specific measures are possible following detailed analysis of a given community's internal and external relations. Additionally, as Kabeer has argued, gender-sensitive policies must reflect an understanding that gender-specific needs and interests between women and men who belong to the same country, race, and/or social class may conflict, despite their intersecting needs and interests and similar life experiences. Poverty eradication policies and strategies are also dependent on critical analyses of the political economy of class, markets, and work processes. For example, the incorporation of women in the labour market is often insufficient to generate an income that allows them to escape poverty. Such is often the case with participation in the informal sector and lower levels of formal labour hierarchies.

An important factor in policy design is the unit of analysis through which to view and implement policy decisions. Debate begins at the theoretical level but it has clear practical implications. The abundant literature on women and gender and development that has appeared since the 1970's has made considerable use of the household as a unit of analysis. This has proved to be a useful and strategic starting point for understanding the significance of gender relations and unequal distributions of resources and power. We will briefly point out distinctions between three different views of the household and explore their implications for the analyses of poverty and the formulation of poverty eradication policies.

- The orthodox neo-classical approach tends to view the household as a harmonious unit within which decisions regarding consumption, the division of labour, and labour market participation are made without apparent tensions among household members. In its most extreme version, an altruist household head (assumed to be male) essentially guarantees not only maximisation of household utility but also "helps families ensure their members against disasters and other consequences of uncertainty". Thus, poverty eradication measures informed by this model assume that there is no need to conceptualise separately the experiences of women living in poverty because their needs are automatically and harmoniously addressed by an altruist household head. This is exemplified by the social investment funds mentioned earlier. Additionally, the existence of a high proportion of female-headed households across countries is foreign to this conceptualisation.
- The household has been viewed as the locus of tension and struggle where unequal power relations between women and men are manifested. This approach questions the notion of the family as an harmonious unit,

suggesting that it must be understood "as a location of production and redistribution". Without denying that families "also encompass strong emotional ties", it emphasises "the nature of work people do in the family and their control over the products of their labour". Thus, using this approach, poverty eradication measures must take into consideration the division of labour within the household and the gender-related resource distribution which affect gender relations. For example, because women tend to use a higher proportion of their earnings on children and household expenses, poverty eradication measures that increase women's income are more likely to have a positive effect on family well-being than if they are addressed to men.

- An intermediate approach conceptualises the household as the locus of both tension and cooperation. It interprets the family as a contradictory institution through which power, affective relations, and resource distribution are played out at the micro level. Amartya Sen's household bargaining model, which emphasises the "cooperative conflicts" that characterise household relations, typifies this approach. In this framework, the process of bargaining depends upon a series of characteristics that define the relative strengths and/or weaknesses of different household members. Within this approach, actions can be taken to improve women's bargaining position. Hence, it is useful in terms of providing guidelines for gender-sensitive poverty eradication measures, such as those geared to increasing women's self-esteem and autonomy, improving their health, decreasing their work load, and ensuring their greater access and control over resources.

**Women as Agents of Change**

The task of engendering poverty eradication measures must not be limited to locating the household as *the* centre of analysis. It must focus on the different levels at which poverty producing processes are at work. In each case, however, our conceptual approach to understanding gender relations are key to the design of appropriate policy and action. Additionally, in all cases it is critical to emphasise the role of women's agency in these processes.

The 1980s and 1990s have provided numerous illustrations of the key roles played by women in daily survival during periods of crises and deteriorating living standards. For example, we have witnessed the establishment of a growing number of women's organisations focusing on "the politics of needs" and on survival strategies adopted by the poor as a result of structural adjustment. Taken together, they provide a compelling picture of a fierce struggle to survive in a period of adverse economic conditions. In this context, the visibility of poor women's actions and work have become prominent. Women's roles in these processes provide a foundation on which poverty eradication measures must rely. As Dreze and Sen have argued for the case of India, "the agency of women as a force for change is one of the most neglected aspects of the development literature". This neglect must not continue. There is a need to document the ways in which poverty is experienced by women and men in order to engender poverty eradication measures. Quantitative and qualitative methodologies, when used together, can be important tools for such a task. However, when either methodology is used in isolation, the result is most often an incomplete analysis of poverty processes. For example, disaggregating statistics on poverty according to gender provides a limited view of the extent to which women are affected by poverty. Significant qualitative dimensions of poverty, such as stress, poor self-esteem, and dependency elude quantification yet they also provide an incomplete picture of poverty without supplementary quantitative data. Furthermore, it is important to note that because poverty concerns health, shelter, education, security, access to productive resources, and other aspects of living standards, statistics that are more than two or three years old are often not useful to inform policy.

The extent to which poverty eradication measures can work through the market and adjust to market criteria is an important consideration in the formulation of gender sensitive-policies. Economic growth is a necessary but insufficient condition for poverty eradication. Structural changes that increase the access of poor women and men to productive resources as well as investment in social reproduction, redistribution, and more equitable distribution are necessary to end poverty.

The World Bank has recognised that gender inequality cannot be eradicated through market forces alone and that it is "essential that public policies work to compensate for market failures" so as to "equalise opportunities between women and men and redirect resources to those investments with the highest social returns". Thus, although still centering its criteria around the notion of "returns," the Bank has recognised the need to design policies that can improve women's entitlements and capabilities. The World Bank has also argued that "governments can no longer afford not to invest in women" because the evidence on "the high private and social returns to investment in women and girls cannot be ignored". The Bank has also pointed out that the "persistent inequalities between men and women lead to lower productivity and growth". These arguments, although important, emphasise a functionalist approach to gender equality based on market criteria; they typify the "efficiency approach" and stress the need to improve women's lives as a way of maximising "the wealth of nations". In so doing, they tend to ignore gender relations and institutions as well as the factors that improve women's bargaining power.

Thus, policy makers and practitioners must be wary of strategies that prioritise market-dominated policies for poverty eradication because they are unlikely to eradicate the gendered dimensions of poverty, unless they are accompanied by measures focusing on entitlements, choices, rights and capabilities. As illustrated, even though market processes assist the poor to generate income, it has often been under conditions of low wages, occupational hazards, and poor working conditions that do not eradicate poverty. International development organisations are in strategic positions to formulate and influence policies and implement programmes/projects that promote the eradication of poverty in general and its gendered dimensions in particular.

**Role of UN**

Since the first 1975 United Nations Conference on the Decade for Women. As it has been said, "we have moved from seeing women as victims to needing them to save the world". During the past two decades, women's issues have been at the forefront of social change. Yet poverty, with its gender dimensions, has far from disappeared. In this chapter we argue that to successfully eradicate poverty it is imperative to focus on gender as a category separate from the category "women" in poverty eradication measures. Consequently, it is important to look not only at women in isolation but at women in relation to men and institutions. This approach is implicit in the World Social Summit's "Copenhagen Declaration and Programme of Action."

Given the current emphasis on democratisation and investment in civil societies, it is important to focus on the factors that can contribute to this process. Most countries face one of the most potentially explosive contradictions of our times, namely, increasing economic and social polarisation, partially as a result of the dynamics of the market within an increasingly global economy. This is happening at a time when emphasis on human rights, equality, higher levels of education, and expanding information systems are the cornerstones of "the new civil society" and of democratic institutions. A significant proportion of the literature focusing on growing inequalities indicates that gender, class, racial, and other types of inequalities must be addressed.

# 6

# National Policy

This chapter has thrust on substantial set of focus group data from 1987-88 in Matlab Thana in Bangladesh, where the Family Planning and Health Services Project had been underway since 1977. That project was highly successful in increasing family planning acceptance, and provided a rich research base for studying the diffusion of family planning and its effects. The 1987-88 study involved 36 focus groups involving fieldworkers, community women, husbands, educated women, and community leaders. Planning programs sometimes reach beyond their intended targets, namely to young, unmarried women. Qualitative information from the recollections of a rural Bangladeshi woman and focus group discussions are utilized. Diffusion of family planning concepts among this unexpected audience in rural Matlab Bangladesh, was first described to the authors by Shamiran, a Matlab woman. Her story retold events that occurred during the initial arrival of the Matlab community-based family planning worker in the late 1970s. Shamiran and a friend, unmarried pre-teens at that time, became curious about the nature of the worker's visit and hid outside the older women's homes to hear the worker's messages. The girls inquired about the meaning of the information from an aunt; the aunt helped them understand what they overheard.

Shamiran's story indicated that contraceptive information was not widely available to young, unmarried women in the community. Yet, her words described the family planning field worker as more than a vehicle for contraceptive information. The family planning worker was a representative of modern ideas and an inspiration for a new consciousness about reproductive decision making. She set an example for female mobility, employment, and modern dress, and through her work legitimized the use of contraception and communicated new ideas about family size norms. These new concepts strongly appealed to Shamiran.

After the worker's visits, the newly acquired information was duly passed on, into a network of female peers. In the process, a group of women in their most impressionable years were reached with information about contraceptive methods and new ideas of reproductive behavior. Shamiran expounded upon these new ideas to her more conservative and demure companion, and made them a topic of conversation with her peers. Individuals who are knowledgeable about the Matlab community have confirmed that the patterns described in the story coincide with their own recollections. Four focus group discussions were designed to further explore these issues; newly married, young women were asked to discuss their experiences in the late 1980s. Additionally, other community women were asked a set of questions about young women. The data were derived from a study conducted in 1987-88 in the Maternal Child Health and Family Planning Project in Matlab, Bangladesh. Findings revealed that the diffusion of new ideas about family size and contraception were anchored in perceptions of broader social change.

The themes from Shamiran's recollections of events from the previous decade were both reaffirmed and broadened. All of the focus group participants were aware of the family planning worker's visit to their neighborhood and families, and most talked about a growing awareness and curiosity concerning the worker's visits. The typical first impression of the worker was that she was a doctor who gave out pills, injections, saline solution and other medicines. It was also clear that the community-based worker had become a role model, and that her visits stimulated a pattern of gradual learning and growing consciousness about the worker's family planning tasks. Data also indicated that, for some participants, understanding of the worker's family planning functions began prior to the onset of menstruation; for others menarche was the threshold. Older women commented that the young girls were learning much from the presence of the worker. It was clear that the community worker's presence in the village set in motion a process of observation, questioning and even direct exchanges with the worker. The young, recently married women themselves credited her for their growing awareness of the concept and meaning of family planning. In contrast, the older women acknowledged that they had not had such opportunities to learn about this topic. The discussions suggest that not only information and knowledge about contraceptive techniques and how to gain access to them is communicated; the very "thinkability" that women can control their reproductive live was also being established.

**Fertility Control**

The receptivity of older women to the idea of fertility control, and their discussion of these topics were also important factors in the diffusion process. Contraceptive prevalence and family planning discussions were increasing among adult women; these increases contributed significantly to the diffusion of new ideas to young, unmarried women. Almost all of the young, recently married focus group participants knew a contraceptive user within their family or bari prior to their marriage. Data also showed that the diffusion of family planning information and ideas occurred within a context where the underlying assumptions and values of reproductive change were encountering increasing approval and where their implications for the status of women were beginning to be perceived.

Most participants indicated they had discussed the worker's activities with their girl friends before their marriages. Such discussions continued after marriage, and provided an important mechanism for the diffusion of knowledge about sexual matters and contraception. Because the newly married women were included in conversation with older women and with the family planning worker, she provided an important source of information to her unmarried peers. The role of the media in communicating new ideas about family size and contraception has also emerged as a central theme. While the community worker, female relatives, peers and other community women were important sources of family planning information, the influences of radios, and even television or printed materials, were also mentioned. Radios were widely available in the villages at the time the study took place, and in 1987 family planning broadcasts were regular and noticed by the young women interviewed.

This undoubtedly contributed to their knowledge and awareness as the young women stated that they had heard a variety of programs sponsored by the government family planning program, covering the importance of limiting childbearing, that the two-child family is a happy family, what methods are available, how methods work, etc. This chapter suggests that the Matlab family planning worker acted as a catalyst in the diffusion of new ideas and information to young, unmarried women who were not targeted by the formal program strategies of the Matlab project.

**Media Campaign**

Both the presence of the worker and the media campaign provided a stimulus for conversations in which new knowledge and ideas were processed through interaction among peers and family members. The basic conclusion of the chapter is that the Matlab family planning program is inadvertently reaching an audience that was not targeted by the formal program strategy; girls and unmarried young women were beginning to be inducted into the culture of contraception as part of their normal process of socialization.

**Women's Lives in Transition**

In contrast to earlier demographic and social science predictions, a fertility decline is well underway in Bangladesh. This chapter explores factors related to the decline using a qualitative data set collected through focus group sessions. The basic argument presented is that the fertility transition in Bangladesh has multiple determinants, many of which are not easily studied by examining macro-level data.

Dialogue with rural women of different ages in the Matlab communities indicates that multiple dimensions of Matlab women's lives are being transformed, and together these changes explain the interest in family limitation and spacing. The presence of a strong program is a major contributing influence in the demographic transition, but social and economic changes, as well as a new mental outlook, new ideas and orientations, also play a meaningful role. Changes are subtle and have not iv affected everyone equally, yet their influence has emerged as a pervasive theme in these discussions.

Important components of the transition involve changes in contraceptive use and family size norms. The data show that family planning has become a frequent topic of conversation and that women are aware of widespread contraceptive use in their communities, and the onset of fertility decline. Women explain that lower fertility benefits them individually and also benefits their families. They believe that using contraceptives, even with their side effects, is preferable to bearing multiple children as their mothers did. Women are also aware of broader changes that are affecting their lives in areas that are conventionally considered demand-side determinants of fertility decline-economic and social changes.

With regards to economic factors, the cost of living is perceived to be increasing. Women speak about the fact that their families have less land than their parents and attribute this change to population growth, land erosion, or the distress sale of land. In a society where subsistence agriculture is still the dominant means of livelihood, decreased land holding implies food shortages and increasing problems in providing for their families. The rising cost of providing for children's needs is also a major concern for women. Women speak of providing for their children beyond the basic necessities of food and clothing; they must be raised to their fullest potential by investing in their future. Likewise, there is an increasing interest in sending both boys and girls to school. Although education is associated with significant expenditures for many families, women recognize that the future of their children rests with employment in the formal sector of the economy, and that education is a major precondition for securing such employment.

**Dowry System**

Among important social changes are the dowry system, changes in family relations, women's emerging sense of self-esteem and freedom, and overall modernization. Women associate dowries with an increasing financial burden and link the cost to childbearing; high dowry costs are perceived as reasons for limiting births. Women in Matlab communities also perceive that family relations are not following the old patterns. Data indicate that the role of parents and parents-in-law have become weakened, conjugal bonds are stronger, family structures are changing, intergenerational wealth flows are beginning to reverse, and young wives are believed to have a degree of influence that defies tradition. Moreover, women are beginning to perceive themselves as worthy individuals, capable of thinking and acting independently, and deserving to enjoy at least some of the pleasures of modern life. There is agreement among the younger and older focus group participants that the younger women are even freer than those over thirty. The freedom to delay the onset of childbearing is a central element in this transition. It is also clear that women not only see their own lives in transition, they perceive the world around them to be in a process of change to which they attach the label of modernity. New modes of transport, electricity and the media have reached the villages, more schools are being built, and more markets exist than in the past. Exposure to a world beyond the boundaries of traditional rural communities brings new ideas, including signs of the orientations and values of a commercialized, consumer society. Women have begun to focus on their own well-being and are trying to escape from what some perceive as the drudgery that characterized the life of their mothers. They want to be part of the commercial culture that is emerging around them. Within these aspirations many children are viewed as "botheration", and the use of contraception becomes an important mechanism for attaining at least a small share of the attractions of modern life.

The role of the Matlab MCH and family planning program, especially the community-based worker in bringing about the transition in women's lives is also discussed. Data reveal that women often view the worker as a trusted friend, someone they can rely on to help them overcome fears of methods and mediate disputes about family planning with relatives. The worker has gone far beyond simply providing access to methods; indeed, she has helped women put reproductive decisions in the "calculus of rational choice", influenced their family size preferences, and served as a role model for modernization. The media, via repeated messages about family planning, has also influenced women although not quite to the extent of the worker.

The conclusion suggests that the fertility transition should be viewed as a consequence of the forces of both supply and demand, even though the demand-side determinants are much smaller and different in nature than major structural transformations stipulated by conventional demographic theory. Further, women are aware of the changes around them, are conscious and deliberate actors in the fertility transition; the program agents and media help them to escape pre-established cultural scripts. The original intent of the proposal to analyze the focus group data collected in Matlab in 1987-88 had been to explore the broader effects of family planning for women's lives and to establish a linkage between program management and these larger effects of the program on women's status. Much of the analysis followed the original intent of examining the effect of family planning on women's lives. Major efforts were put into coding data for analysis utilizing a computer program for qualitative analysis, Ethnograph. Focus group transcripts from sessions with community women (as opposed to sessions conducted with the Matlab workers) were coded along several variables relating to the effect of family planning on women's lives. The codes were entered into the computer program, and printouts of transcript segments reflecting each of the codes are now available. The code sheet for these variables. However, given the new directions, additional coding following more conventional lines of qualitative analysis.

Typical of qualitative work, the Matlab focus group study produced an unexpected research lead, which makes a genuinely new and significant contribution to the field. It showed that the Matlab project affected not only the so-called eligible couples, but also had an effect on young unmarried women, even little girls. With the exception of the work by Alauddin and VanLandingham, the importance of a focus on the young had not been discussed for Bangladesh. "Diffusion of the Culture of Contraception: Program Effects on Young Women in Rural Bangladesh", traces these effects and interprets them in light of the literature on diffusion of innovation. The chapter was accepted by Studies in Family

Planning and has been revised in response to the suggestions by the reviewers. It will be published in the January/February 1995 issue of Studies.

"Women's Lives in Transition, a Qualitative Analysis of the Fertility Decline in Bangladesh". This chapter has also taken on a slightly different focus than originally intended, but the outcome warrants the endeavor. Reading the recent literature on Bangladesh and especially the volume by Cleland et al. The Determinants of Reproductive Change in Bangladesh reconfirmed the importance and uniqueness of the qualitative data collected in Matlab. An analysis of these qualitative data shows a slightly different picture than what Cleland et al. conclude based on analysis of available demographic research and statistical indicators.

Cleland et al. conclude that in Bangladesh, the influence of family planning programs and policies accounts for the onset of fertility decline. While the influence of the program is indeed strong, (as one would expect given that the data come from Matlab), the data also show social and economic change as well as modernizing trends to be important factors affecting decisions to limit family size and use of contraception. While these changes may be objectively small, they amount to life-transforming experiences in the perceptions of the women involved in the transition.

The concept of diffusion has assumed prominence in recent discussions of the fertility transition and reproductive change, although its relevance to the field had of course been indicated earlier. In the most general sense, diffusion refers to a process whereby new ideas, information, practices or technology are disseminated through a variety of mechanisms that affect attitudes and behaviors at local, national and international levels. One of the central arguments of the diffusion literature has been to emphasize the possible independent role of changing ideas and aspirations in enhancing the fertility transition.

Programs deliberately and consciously direct contraceptive information, "motivation" and services at specific populations with whom they interact through personal or impersonal communication. New ideas knowledge and practices are then spread further as they are passed on to others through informal social networks consisting, for example, of family members or peers. In this chapter we show that as ideas and information spread, they reach not only people the program intends to reach, but others as well. This phenomenon has been noted earlier. In the Taichung experiment of the 1960s, IUD acceptance spread to areas where no formal efforts were made to recruit acceptors. Similarly, the interventions initiated within the Matlab project in Bangladesh have some influence on women in the project's comparison area as well. The so-called condom gap in Bangladesh has revealed that contraceptives intended for the public sector program have found their way across the border into Myanmar. In these examples, the spread of ideas and practices or technology crossed geographic boundaries. The key point here is that family planning programs can act as the stimulus that sets in motion the spread of new ideas, information, beliefs, behaviors, and even technology beyond formally targeted audiences. Diffusion effects may be both planned or unanticipated. This chapter describes the social interaction by which new ideas and information spread to a very young audience that was not intended to be reached. Such unanticipated effects became visible in the course of a qualitative study in Matlab, Bangladesh which showed that the presence of the community-based family planning worker had an effect on young, unmarried women and even on little girls.

The potential effect of family planning programs on younger women has been noted in studies of family planning in India and Turkey. Both of these authors present evidence of the indirect effect of programmatic efforts on the young. Policy discussions and related family planning literature on Bangladesh, by contrast, have exclusively focused on married women of reproductive age. Given the predominantly traditional and conservative nature of Bangladeshi society, where the idea of family planning has been until recently controversial and the level of demand for fertility regulation uncertain, such focus was appropriate.

What has been missed, however, is that ideational change, set in motion through the formal family planning program and other modernizing trends, has reached young women whose age and unmarried status requires that they be modest and, at least in theory, protected from knowledge about sexuality and contraception. When new ideas about fertility regulation reach young, unmarried women in the years preceding the onset of sexuality and childbearing, their influence on future family size norms and contraceptive behavior is potentially significant. The insights into these unanticipated diffusion effects were stimulated by a serendipitous discovery made in the course of a focus-group study examining the relationship between women's status and family planning.

In Matlab, Bangladesh, Shamiran, one of the staff members who facilitated focus-group discussions and who had grown up in the Matlab treatment area, vividly remembered the arrival of the community based family planning worker in her local village ten years earlier when she was still unmarried. Her story suggested a fascinating pattern of how new ideas about contraception and norms regarding family size were beginning to reach young women prior to their marriage. We recorded it in detail and adjusted the design of the focus-group study to explore these issues further. We begin the chapter with Shamiran's story and an interpretation of the context within which it occurred.

Story telling is not usually considered a methodological tool for the study of family planning or the diffusion of new ideas. However, this method is gaining increasing recognition as an important approach in anthropology, sociology and in the feminist literature. The information contained in a story can emerge in the course of participant observation, or in in-depth interviews; its objective is to capture how respondents themselves portray a series of incidents and attach meaning to them. We consider it important to tell Shamiran's story because it shows the path through which we gained insight into a diffusion process that has remained largely unrecognized in the literature. It allows us to witness how one woman remembers learning about birth control and to note the circumstances within which such learning occurred. Subsequent sections of the chapter present findings from a focus-group study examining the perspectives and recollections of young women a decade later, when the program was more established in the community.

These findings both reaffirm and broaden the themes from Shamiran's recollections of events from the previous decade. In addition to the varied and complex contribution of the family planning worker, and of social and familial networks, the role of the media in communicating new ideas about family size and contraception emerges as a central theme. The data also show that the diffusion of new ideas about family size and contraception is anchored in perceptions of broader social change. Shamiran's story or the unanticipated effects of family planning diffusion in the late 1970s.

The incidents described in the story occurred in the late 1970s in one of the villages where the Matlab family planning project had selected and trained local women to function as community-based outreach workers. These villages are in a remote part of southern Bangladesh, accessible mainly by river transport, dominated by fishing and agriculture and marked by poverty and an essentially stagnant economic base. They are characterized by a conservative, Muslim culture where female literacy is low and where young, unmarried women lead a life of relative seclusion from exposure to outsiders, particularly men. In the late 1970s, exposure to radios and other forms of communication was minimal. Until 1975 this area had been exposed to family planning information and services through the formal government program, whose impact upon the rural population was marginal. In 1977 a special contraceptive distribution project undertaken by the International Centre for Diarrhoeal Disease Research (ICDDR,B) was reorganized into the Matlab Maternal and Child Health and Family Planning Project. The impact of this project on contraceptive prevalence was immediate and sustained, rising from 7 percent at the inception of the reorganized project to 20 percent within three months and to 30 percent by the end of 1978, the approximate time when the events described in the following story took place. As described elsewhere, the women who were appointed as community-based family planning workers caused an uproar among many villagers when they first began to make their household visits. They were considered the incarnation of a devil that appeared to bring misfortune to the villages, or were rudely compared to bitches in heat who chased after men.

Despite such devastating comments, workers succeeded in establishing their trustworthiness and credibility within a relatively short period of time, and the Matlab project has been hailed as an example of the kind of program impact that can be achieved despite the existence of major socio-economic constraints.

We see Mukti's Ma as someone who visits the married women in Shamiran's bari on a regular basis, and who appears to be a well-accepted and welcome visitor.

The story is based on the initial conversation with Shamiran and a detailed follow-up interview with her to reconstruct the events that had occurred a decade earlier: One day in the mango and jack fruit orchard Shamiran and Bani, two young girls of 18 and 19 years, were talking and laughing among themselves. They had heard that the previous night a marriage proposal had come for Bani. Her parents were going to consider it seriously. The girls were talking about the would-be husband of Bani and laughing. Suddenly, Shamiran saw a lady with a colorful sari and a bag on her shoulder. She entered into a house. After some time, they saw the lady coming out of that bari and entering Shamiran's bari. Bani said: "Who is she? Why is she going to different houses?" Shamiran answered:

The two young girls went to the bari and found the lady was talking with Shamiran's aunt in a low voice. A few other women of the bari were surrounding her. Shamiran and Bani approached the group but Shamiran's aunt immediately said: "Go away, you are not supposed to join the discussion of older women." Shamiran had noticed that the lady had stopped talking when she saw Bani and Shamiran. The two girls left, but became extremely curious about the discussion and the role of the lady. Shamiran could identify her: "She is Mukti's Ma (women in rural Bangladesh are typically referred to as the mother of one of her children) from another bari of the village. She used to come to our bari previously as well. But why is she so dressed up and talking in such a low voice? "Shamiran could not forget the lady.

The next day Shamiran went to her aunt pleading: "Please aunt, tell me what is the secret of Mukti's Ma? What was she telling you?" The aunt, a young woman, was quite friendly with Shamiran. Shamiran held the hand of her aunt, pleading: "Please tell me," but the aunt replied: "No, when you will be married, then I will tell you."

Shamiran rushed to Bani telling her: "This is something to do with the married women, can you guess?" Bani also became excited. But they could not reach any conclusion about Mukti Ma's work. Finally, Shamiran said: "The next time Mukti's Ma comes, we will listen to their conversation." Bani was hesitant: "No, no, we should not do that. The aunt will mind." But Shamiran insisted: "Nobody will know, we will hide inside the room and listen. Please do not say no." Bani then was convinced and they started waiting for Mukti's Ma.

Finally the day came when Mukti's Ma returned to Shamiran's bari. Secretly Shamiran and Bani entered the room and carefully listened to the conversation. It was difficult to hear, because the women were talking in a low voice. First they heard Mukti's Ma asking about the date of the women's last period. Then she gave them some medicine and explained how to use it, telling them that if anyone had any problem then they should inform her immediately. Shamiran was so excited that she came out of the room and went to her aunt, saying: "We have seen what Mukti's Ma said to you and gave you. We know the story." The aunt said: "Didn't I tell you not to listen?", but Shamiran replied: "Now I know." Then the aunt said: "Well, since you came to know already, listen: Those medicines are for controlling childbirth. If you do not want any more children then you can have those.

When you will want another child then stop using those medicines and you can have the baby. You should not discuss these with anybody. When you will be married off Mukti's Ma will go to you or I will tell you ok? No more questioning, go." Shamiran was amazed at her discovery. She went to Bani and explained everything. Bani said: "You should not say all these things, I feel shy." But Shamiran and Bani continued to discuss the topic several times. Shamiran said: "I think Mukti's Ma is doing a good job. I will have those medicines when I will be married off. Bani said: "How dare you talk like that before marriage." But Shamiran replied: "I think you should also think about these medicines, because you are going to get married soon." Then Shamiran went to school and discussed everything with the other young girls of the village.

Some of them knew about Mukti's Ma and her work. Some did not. But everybody was interested in talking to her. One girl said: Look at her, she wears her sari so nicely, and goes to different baris. My sister told me she earns a good amount of money." Others said: "But my father and grandmother said she is not a good lady." Shamiran replied: "Grandmothers and fathers are always behind the times.

Some girls said: "Yes, we should have this medicine, so we will not have so many problems with too many children. With few children we will be able to keep our sari clean and nice." Everybody laughed together.

Given the norms of female seclusion, women - especially those with social status and prestige - would not normally visit other baris, certainly not without the accompaniment of a male relative. Thus, the very presence of a single woman from a good family, wearing a burkah which covers her from head to toe, signaled a departure from tradition and the possibility of excitement. The fact that the older women attempt to hide information about the worker's purposes from the young women fits established patterns of decency, whereby topics related to sexuality are not to be discussed with elders. Young, recently married women in the bari or peers are often the source of sexual information; mothers do not usually transmit such information to their daughters. To anyone who has done fieldwork in rural South Asia, it will not be surprising that the young women succeed without much difficulty in their plans to secretly overhear the worker's conversation with the older women during her next visit to the bari.

Privacy or secrecy are not easily assured in houses were walls are thin or consist of no more than a bamboo mat, where windows are open, and enclosed spaces small and cramped. It is clear from the story that contraceptive information was not widely available to young, unmarried women in the community, although some had learned about the family planning worker's role earlier than Shamiran. The ideas represented by the family planning worker exercise a strong appeal to Shamiran, who begins proclaiming the values of change to her more conservative and demure companion, and engages in a set of conversations with her peers. In quoting the final passage from Shamiran's story, Pollak and Watkins conclude that Conversations such as the one between Shamiran and her friends expose culture.. in the process of change...(T)he accumulation of such conversations is likely to establish a commonality of perception that these new contraceptive techniques are available, that their use is preferable to a life of continual childbearing and dirty saris, and that their use is not only within the calculus of conscious choice but would be acceptable to their friends. Shamiran's story allows us to witness the multifaceted dimensions of the diffusion process.

The presence of the family planning worker in the community constitutes the "pebble in the pond" that generates a new consciousness about reproductive decision making, provides information about the means of contraception, legitimates its use, and communicates new ideas about family size norms.

Older women, such as married aunts, who were practicing contraception or merely took part in the conversations with the worker - acted as a reference group essential in unlocking the secrets behind the worker's visit and in affirming new norms about contraceptive use. The newly acquired information does not remain a secret, but passes on into the network of female peers, who examine and evaluate what has been learned within a context of some prior knowledge about family planning and its controversial nature in the community. In the process, a group of women in their most impressionable years are reached with information about contraceptive methods and new aspects of reproductive behavior in ways that were entirely unanticipated by the official diffusion strategies of the Matlab project. These strategies were focused entirely on interpersonal exchanges with married women of reproductive age with a strong preference for waiting until a woman had her first child. It is important to ask to what extent this story truly reflects the experience of Shamiran herself and of other young, unmarried women in the community.

While inaccuracy in some of the detail is to be expected in any interviewing process that reconstructs events from a decade earlier, individuals who are knowledgeable about the Matlab community have confirmed that the patterns described in the story coincide with their own recollections. As Shamiran's story revealed, for some young women learning about the worker's functions might have occurred within a context of personal, or parental disapproval of the use of contraception. Since the initial community response to the presence of the Matlab family planning worker was hostile, not all young women would have experienced exposure to the new information as positive or enlightening.

Moreover, cross-pressures might have been generated by a contrast in the general tenor of the debate among peers and parental responses to the worker's presence. It should also be noted, however, that the young women described in this story come from relatively well-to-do and more modern families because formal schooling for girls is not affordable to the poor and not necessarily considered desirable by the more traditional families. Thus, girls who do not attend school would have more limited exposure to peers. The diffusion of contraceptive ideas to young unmarried women in the late 1980s. When we heard Shamiran's recollection of her encounters with the community based family planning worker, four focus-group sessions with young, recently married women were added to the study, and a set of questions about young women were incorporated into the guidelines for the sessions with other community women. In order to explore the possible influence of the community worker's presence on adolescent women, we initially contemplated interviewing unmarried girls in their teens. This idea was quickly rejected. In a society which values female seclusion and modesty, especially in young, unmarried women, participation in a focus-group discussion would not have been allowed or might have had negative repercussions. Interviewing recently married women, asking them to reflect upon the years prior to their marriage and upon the role of the community worker in their lives at that time, seemed a more feasible approach. The considerable difficulties involved in arranging sessions with young, recently married women, which we discuss below, reaffirmed the wisdom of not seeking to interview unmarried ones.

The day preceding the focus-group session, one of the moderators (herself a resident of Matlab with considerable experience in arranging other data collection activities in the local community) identified appropriate participants together with the family planning worker and sought the permission of older relatives. After much explaining, she was usually able to obtain such permission. However, it was not uncommon to find that consent had been withdrawn the next day.

Since it is a requirement of focus-group research that participants assemble in one place, some of the young women must leave their own household and their bari in order to do so. Even though one of the moderators would always accompany them, elder women in the family were hesitant to grant permission. These circumstances reflect the extent of social control exerted on recently married women and the limited exposure they have to influences coming from beyond the boundaries of their husband's families, their own parents, and their bari. In one instance, resentment against one of the family planning workers who was known as haughty and unsupportive of community women, especially when they needed help with side effects or other problems, also complicated the process of obtaining permission. A total of 15 recently married women participated in these special focus-group sessions. Their average age was 16.7 years; they had been married between 6 months and a year. Six participants had no formal education; the mean years of schooling was three. The husbands of these young women worked in agriculture or fishing (6), in service (4) as shopkeepers (2), as a day laborer (1), a tailor (1), or was a student (1). We refer to these focus-group participants as the young, recently married women.

The sessions lasted several hours and were typically interrupted by relatives who came to call one of the participants asking her to return home. In one session, for example, a female relative came and told two of the participants: "Your husbands have come from the field, immediately go home or your husband will beat you". The session was interrupted for several hours, to allow these two women to return home and attend to their domestic responsibilities.

The analysis has excluded any reference to answers produced under such circumstances. Participants in the other three sessions were slightly older and had been married somewhat longer, which seemed to make it easier for them to express their views in front of strangers. The focus-group study of older women consisted of 17 sessions with participants between the age of 20 and 45 from different villages of the Matlab project area. Thirteen of these sessions were comprised of women with no or minimal level of education. Their husbands worked predominantly in agriculture, but also as owners of local shops or small businesses, as teacher, local priest, or craftsman. The participants of four remaining sessions had a least an eighth grade education; their husbands worked in farming, business, as village doctor or in a service position. We refer to these focus-group participants as the older women. Focus-group sessions were taped and translated verbatim by Bangladeshi translators. Quotations from these transcripts are extensively utilized in presenting findings. Except for minor editorial changes, quotations have not been altered from their original translations.

As was true for Shamiran and her peers in the late 1970s, the process of social interaction by which diffusion of contraceptive information and ideas to young, unmarried women takes place in the 1980s involves the family planning worker; mothers, female relatives as well as other community women; and peers.

The role of the media, however, constitutes a departure from the previous pattern. Below, we discuss each of these influences in turn.

*The role of the family planning worker*: All of the young, recently married focus-group participants were aware of the community health worker's visit to their neighborhood and their families. However there were differences in the extent to which they understood her family planning role. The shy and very young participants in one focus-group knew only that the worker visited their families. They indicated that they did not understand anything about her purpose, did not overhear any conversation, and did not discuss any of these issues with anyone prior to their marriage. Reticence to acknowledge knowing about contraceptive use may have influenced their responses to our questions, but obviously, not all the unmarried young women, especially not those who are very young, learn about family planning prior to their marriage. Participants in the other three groups, however, talked about a growing awareness and curiosity concerning the worker's visits.

The first impression typically was of the worker as a doctor, who gave out pills, injections, saline solution and other medicines. They also realized that "she was a doctor for mothers and children, not for fathers". In one of the sessions, participants remembered talking to the worker and being extremely impressed by her. Undeterred by the negative comments of some villagers, they decided that they liked her, and began wishing they might one day become such a "doctor" themselves:

> First we feared Mahmuda and gazed at her when she moved from place to place.
>
> We thought, if we could only become a person like her.
>
> I also thought a lot. I asked her how she applies her knowledge as a doctor, and requested her to take me along. She replied: "What will I do with you, if you come along? Will you be able to practice like me?"
>
> I insisted: "If I carry your bag, and move with you, one day I will be able to become a doctor like you?"

The community-based worker has become a role model, although initially some of young girls feared her because she gave injections. The notion that she is a doctor is reinforced by the considerable maternal-and-child health components of the Matlab project, especially in the later years of the 1980s. The worker's visits stimulated a pattern of gradual learning and growing consciousness about the worker's family planning tasks.

> I was very curious and used to ask Mahmuda (the worker) every day what is this, and what is that, ultimately I came to know.
>
> I heard Mahmuda advising women about the methods that suit them and saw aunts taking methods. We youths discussed among ourselves that as the babies are born, Mahmuda gives different things. We gathered by the side of Mahmuda and

> asked her what is the thing that she holds on. We ran way when Mahmuda raised her hand to give us a splash.
>
> Our curiosity increased and we started listening to her conversation with mothers, sisters, and aunts.
>
> I and Nilufer listened to the conversation and saw her handing over medicine to a young lady, whom we used to call sister. We two started observing her (wanting to know) what happens to her. Why is she taking medicine? Nilufer one day asked her about the medicine. She said: "You will not understand, it is for family planning." After some months we came to the conclusion that her belly is not getting fatter bigger. Then we were sure that this is for birth control. As Mukti's Ma is here that is why we have access to adopt family planning. She is coming to our mother, aunt, sister, relatives and neighbors and we have been observing her since our childhood.

As the last quote indicates, the worker is known to some participants from their early childhood on. For some, understanding of the worker's family planning functions begins prior to the onset of menstruation; for others menarche is the threshold:

> I could realize all these (things)from a time when I was not married. Actually you can say when menstruation had not yet started.
>
> I did understand they came to teach our mother about the way of controlling birth.
>
> Then I was not so big, before menstruation had started.
>
> At the age of 10-12 years I understood why they were coming and after menstruation things became more clear.
>
> I understood this at the age of 10/11 years.
>
> We are seeing Mahmuda visiting us with methods since the dawn of our understanding.

While some young focus-group participants acknowledge that their mothers succeeded in preventing them from overhearing their conversations with the worker, the older women acknowledge that girls are learning much from her presence. For example:

> The girls are observing Mahmuda (the worker), who comes to their bari and talks with their mothers, aunts, and sister-in-laws. They quite often listen to what she ways and have learned many things. Then they themselves decide that they will not give birth to many children, and will take contraceptives from the night of marriage.
>
> Many girls specially the newly married girls have learned a lot. There are workers in almost all the villages and most of the women are using contraception. The young girls hear from behind and learn about family planning. They (the young girls) gather and try to listen to Mahmuda and have by now understood almost everything.

These patterns are quite similar to what Shamiran remembered from the late 1970s, although they occur earlier in life for girls in the 1980s. The community worker's presence in the village sets in motion a process of observation, questioning and even direct exchanges with the worker. The young, recently married women themselves credit her for their growing awareness of the concept and meaning of family planning: "If we would not have seen Mukti's Ma during our early age, we do not think that we could realize what family planning is or how it could be useful to us". They acknowledge the significance of this learning for their later life: "Yes, we also then thought we will be practicing family planning later during our time," or "the root of the decision was founded then." By contrast, the older women acknowledge that they did not have such opportunities:

> "Our mothers and aunts did never discuss family planning and they were not visited by family planning doctors. So, we couldn't learn anything."
>
> Precisely what is being learned or diffused is, of course a complex issue that cannot be fully answered with the data from this study. The above quotations suggest, though, that not only information and knowledge about contraceptive techniques and how to gain access to them is communicated; the very "thinkability" that women

can control their reproductive lives is also being established. As has been argued in the demographic literature, placing reproductive control within the calculus of rational choice and establishing numeracy about children are important elements in the fertility transition. Has the process of diffusion created ideational change regarding family size preferences? The data from the study of young women are too limited to address this question.

However, there are glimpses indicating that the worker contributes in clarifying the importance of smaller family size in a socio-economic context where there is increasing awareness of the costs involved in raising, educating and marrying children; where population growth has created pressures on the land; and where the demands of an increasingly monetized economy and the overall level of poverty suggest that fewer children are desirable. The following exchange from one of the focus-group sessions with the young, recently married women illustrates the interactive effect of larger social context and the worker's role:

Woman 1: Everybody wants few children.

Woman 2: How one can keep a family small that is the major thought of the people now.

Moderator: How did this attitude grow?

Woman 3: People now understand the benefit and the miseries of small and big families. The poverty compelled people to adopt family planning.

Woman 1: No, listen apa, the government has introduced family planning and the doctors are going house to house and explaining to people again and again, people are also getting interested after continuous listening from the doctor. We now think, well what doctors are telling that is right. We will have fewer children.

Woman 3: More children make so much noise and disturbance to the mother, it is unbearable. This one does not have cloth, that one wants food, another one is sick, and arranging marriage is also a tough thing.

Woman 4: People have now realized that the root of

all miseries lies with too many children. So they like to be happier with fewer numbers of children.

*The role of female relatives and other community women:* The receptivity of the older women to the idea of fertility control, and their discussion of these topics are important factors in the diffusion process. The increase in contraceptive practice (from less than 10 percent to a prevalence rate in the mid forties at the time of the focus-group study) and concomitant increases in family planning discussions among adult women, contribute significantly to the diffusion of new ideas to young, unmarried women. The influence of the worker occurs in a context where mothers, aunts, or sisters-in-law and other community women are practicing and talking about family planning. Almost all of the young, recently married focus-group participants knew a contraceptive user within their family or bari prior to their marriage. They grew up surrounded by a culture of contraception where, as one of the participants phrased it "family planning has become like dal-bhat", (rice and pulses) i.e. something very common. This culture of contraception is defined by the extensive availability, accessibility and use of contraceptive methods, widespread and increasingly open discussion of the topic among adults, and by a structure of beliefs affirming the value of fertility control. These beliefs are shared by the young women and expressed in such statements as:

> It is good to have less children in this age. People who have 5-6 children are facing serious problem in rearing them up. If they have had 2-3 children, they would have become educated and established; or in the acknowledgment that the use of contraception creates greater freedoms for women:
>
> Mothers take Copper T, injection. So repetition of births within a short period is being avoided. Methods are being taken to prevent and delay births, facilitate working and free movement of mothers in all respects.

The diffusion of family planning information and ideas thus occurs within a context where the underlying assumptions and values of reproductive change encounter increasing approval and where their implications for the status of women are beginning to be perceived.

If the above quote sounds like program propaganda, this is precisely because the worker's message has been heard and accepted as valid. As a result, the potential benefits of contraceptive use are appreciated by the young women. However, as will be seen from later quotations, not only positive information about contraceptive use spreads, the negative implications especially about side effects are learned as well.

Obviously, the older women who use contraception are themselves influenced by the presence of the family planning worker and the Matlab project. In fact, the high contraceptive prevalence in the community is in large measure a reflection of the project's activities. As innovations become widely accepted, they are spread through multiple sources. In the evidence presented here, the worker and family members are simultaneous and mutually interactive influences on the young, unmarried women beginning from an early age. The presence of the family planning worker in the community is noticed and observed, but a member of the family, the bari or - as we will discuss later- a peer unlocks the mystery of her visits. Diffusion proceeds despite prevalent norms that unmarried, young women should be excluded from family planning discussions, and despite the fact that some mothers succeed in preventing their daughters from gaining access to contraceptive information. News about contraceptive use involving regular administration of injections, or even home-based IUD insertion is not easily concealed in an environment where privacy does not exist. As one of the young women remarked: "We used to know from people that they use [contraception]. If a couple takes any such method, the news somehow spreads." While norms about excluding young women from access to contraceptive information continue to be strong, the futility of assuring adherence to this norm in daily practice is becoming increasingly apparent.

When mothers take their small children on their lap while talking with the family planning worker, they may miss the point of transition where the young child begins to grasp the content of the conversation. With growing awareness that girls are beginning to learn about contraception, efforts to actually hide the information from them may simply decrease. Thus in the late 1980s when contraceptive use has ceased to be the innovation it had been a decade earlier, girls and unmarried young women are beginning to be inducted into the culture of contraception as part of their normal process of socialization.

**Discussion with peers**

Except for the one group that claimed no knowledge of the worker's family planning function prior to marriage, most of the other participants indicate they discussed the worker's activities with their girl friends:

> We have had discussions with our girl friends of our age. I have told my friends that when methods will be available in our place, we will adopt these. We said we won't take 10 or 12 children. What need is there to have so many children...

Communication patterns in rural Bangladesh are strongly shaped by gender and age. As indicated earlier, family planning is on the whole still considered a sensitive subject between older women and girls or young women. As such communication, is not sanctioned by the norms of traditional culture, especially with mothers, the older women know with less precision what goes on in peer networks. As one participant put it: "(The elders) do not know that the girls know so many things. The young girls do not say anything in front of their mothers or aunts. They talk about it with their friends, newly married sisters and sisters-in-law."

However, as the above quotations illustrate, there are no bars to discussing these topics with girl friends. Such discussion continues after marriage, and provides an important mechanism for the diffusion of knowledge about sexual matters and contraception. As the newly married woman is now included in the conversation with older women and with the family planning worker, she provides an important source of information to her unmarried peers. The role of peers in the diffusion process is multiplied by the fact that an increasing number of girls are allowed to go to school.

This provides them access to a network of peers with whom they would otherwise not have the opportunity to meet and talk. However, because sending girls to school is associated with monetary expenses and other costs, the number of girls who attend school is still limited.

*The influence of the media:* While the community worker, female relatives, peers and other community women are important sources of family planning information, the influence of radios, and even television or printed materials, is also mentioned. The young women hear a variety of programs sponsored by the government family planning program, covering the importance of limiting childbearing, that the two-child family is a happy family, what methods are available, how methods work, etc. For example in the following exchange women indicate a focus on the characteristics of contraceptive methods:

> Moderator: Do you listen to radio programs regularly? What are the programs normally played by the radio?
>
> Woman 1: The radio plays varieties of programs: songs, talks of different people, family planning programs etc.
>
> Moderator: Can you tell me what are the texts of a family planning program?
>
> Woman 2: The texts of a family planning program vary. Sometimes we find that a man has been narrating how he has been able to check the birth of a baby or how a woman has been able to overcome the side effects of Maya Bori etc.
>
> Women 3: One lady says she has been using family planning for six years. She has taken 9 babies and will not take any more now.
>
> Woman 2: Sometime they say about the side-effect of Maya Bori, at the same time they explain the meaning and how the Maya Bori functions.
>
> Woman 1: Apa initially for one or two months are may be some vertigo, some nausea, but after some time it becomes normal. It is the same as injection also.
>
> Woman 4: Copper T is for three years then it is to be removed.

In another group of women, one commented on the motivational aspects of radio programs:

> All the time they say, a son and a daughter is

> enough and they will have peace in the future and there will be no crisis of food, clothings. That's why government has introduced family planning.

Although the interviews do not allow us to identify when the young women began listening to such programs, it seems plausible that this began prior to, and not after, marriage. At the time the focus-group interviews were conducted, radios had become widely available in the villages. They were clearly a stronger influence on these young women than on Shamiran, who grew up at a time when radios were rare and the family planning content of programs limited. In 1987, family planning broadcasts were regular and were noticed by the young women we interviewed. This undoubtedly contributed to their family planning knowledge and awareness. As one participant put it, women "learn from the doctor (that is from the worker) and from radios, and the educated girls learn by themselves." One of the young women indicated that without the presence of the worker in the community and the discussions which ensue, the knowledge obtained from the media remains abstract:

> As she visits us we began understanding that methods are available now and that it is good to take methods. They (CHWs) helped us know and understand that actually methods are of great help to people. She was the one who circulated the message of family planning and made it popular in the community. The radio has been talking, but did not put these things in the hands of the people.

> Another recently married woman however indicated that in her case the learning came specifically from the radio: " No, Mahmuda didn't help me understand. At first, I heard the advertisement in the radio and came to understand the matter."

The older women also acknowledge the influence of the radio. One participant remarks perceptively that it is not always easy to sort out the relative weight of the various sources of information that affect the young women's knowledge of family planning:

> Girls eventually learned about contraceptives. They also indirectly followed Momtaz [the worker]. The

> trend of age made them curious to know about family planning. Often they follow our discussion. We don't exactly know who formally told them about family planning but Momtaz's visits to us and the massive radio programs on family planning certainly and significantly contributed in their learning about family planning methods and its utility and importance. Often they follow our discussion. We don't exactly know from whom they have learned.

**Implications for research and policy**

We have suggested that the Matlab family planning worker acted as a catalyst in the diffusion of new ideas and information to young, unmarried women who were not targeted by the formal program strategies of the Matlab project. The family planning worker was important in the diffusion of information and ideas in the late 1970s when the Matlab project had recently been initiated, and her role continued to be strong in the 1980s in the presence of a stronger media influence and increased acceptance of the culture of contraception within the community. The diffusion process described here is a complex one and does not consist only of simple dyads between the worker and young women.

These are the salient social networks of the young women in these traditional, conservative villages of rural Bangladesh. Thus, "women's gossip" assumes an important influence in the process of demographic change while contact with agents of the family planning program serves as a major impetus for conversations about contraception and family size. Precisely what is being diffused is not as easily specified as the components of the network through which it is being communicated.

Some of the comments made by the young focus-group participants suggest that the program introduced the concept or "thinkability" that women can control their reproductive lives, placing reproductive control within the calculus of rational choice and establishing numeracy of children. Closely related, though worthy of differentiation from the thinkability of reproductive choice, is the legitimacy of fertility regulation. Clearly this is also being communicated both through communication with peers and elders, and through the social identification with the worker as a symbol of modernity. Similarly, the media messages also legitimate fertility regulation as appropriate behavior within a modern lifestyle. Since the data presented here have concentrated on the experience of girls prior to their marriage, the question of whether the means of fertility control are made available in this process of diffusion has limited applicability. Information and knowledge about contraceptive techniques, how they work and even of the side-effects are spreading.

However, the actual availability of methods is not as relevant for young, unmarried women. Of course, it is becoming clear to them that the means are indeed available within the community and will be available to them once they are married. Undoubtedly more controversial and complex is the question of whether the diffusion of new ideas and values regarding family size desires has occurred. A long-standing and continuing debate within the population field surrounds this issue as well as the question of the contribution of program effort to the fertility transition. Much demographic theory and analysis suggest that programs have no effect on family size desires, and that, at best, they mobilize or crystallize latent demand for lower family size.

Our data on the young, unmarried women do not allow us to address this question with depth and conclusiveness. The fact that survey data from both the treatment and the comparison area of the project reveal parallel reductions in family size desires would suggest that preferences have remained unaffected by the Matlab program, or that the government and the Matlab program have had similar effects on family size desires. However, to entirely disavow the influence of diffusion effects on family size desires would misrepresent the voices of focus-group participants, who attribute an influence to the worker that is broader than the mere communication of information, the placing of reproductive behavior within the calculus of rational choice, or the legitimation of these new ideas. The diffusion of family planning ideas to young, unmarried women and the process by which it occurs, is part of a larger configuration of new influences that affect rural, traditional communities in

Bangladesh.

Some of these influences have already been identified above, namely radios, television, and somewhat greater access to educational opportunities, especially for girls. Other changes include some increased exposure to urban employment, improved transportation facilities, increased electrification of rural areas, and the gradual penetration of a commercial economy into the rural sector. In fact, both exposure to the worker and to the media simply not only a confrontation with new ideas about contraception but signify exposure to the influence of modernity as well. These changes do not amount to a socio-structural transformation of the type that is conventionally associated with fertility decline. Nonetheless, they encourage a new outlook on life and engender a set of aspirations which are eminently compatible with the idea and practice of modern birth control.

There are several implications from these findings for both research and policy. The analysis presented here is based on a small, exploratory study pursuing an insight that arose in the course of a larger study. The results presented in this chapter cannot be viewed as definitive or complete evidence on the issue of program effects on the young in Bangladesh. Additional research on the diffusion of contraceptive knowledge, attitudes and aspirations to girls and young, unmarried women would obviously be desirable. It would be especially important to examine whether the female workers in the national, government run program have had similar effects on this audience. However, extreme sensitivity to the vulnerability of young women must be exhibited in such studies to assure that young women do not suffer negative repercussions as a consequence of their participation in the research. The unanticipated benefits that result from the presence of a community based family planning worker in a traditional, rural community have several implications for policy. First, these findings are important in the context of the broader policy debate about the future role of female workers within the national family planning program. There has been much discussion of the role of female workers in the Bangladesh program. With the increased nationwide prevalence of contraceptive use, questions about the need for continued reliance upon female outreach workers have been raised. The findings from this study underscore previous arguments about the significance of the female outreach worker in rural Bangladesh communities. While the data presented here do not allow us to generalize to Bangladesh as a whole, it is highly plausible that some of these effects would occur there as well. Our findings imply that investments in the employment of women as community-based family planning workers may have had important pay-offs beyond what had been expected. While this chapter does not review the multiple roles of female workers in the national program, its findings suggest additional evidence for their critical contribution in rural areas.

The need for programmatic attention to the contraceptive needs of young married women. As Alauddin and VanLandingham have argued, there has not been enough attention to these needs of younger women. From everything we learned in the focus-group discussions, it is clear that the new generation of young women may have great interest in contraceptive use early on in their married lives. We wish to conclude with a caveat. The findings presented here should not be interpreted to imply that similar effects on the younger generation can be expected in all program settings where women are employed as outreach workers. The findings presented here are dependent upon a social context where women's exposure to the outside world is minimal, and where women and especially young, unmarried women lead a life of relative isolation from the larger influences of the community and society.

**The Output**

Bangladesh has provided scholars and population professionals with a double surprise. In contrast to earlier demographic and social science predictions, a fertility decline was initiated in what is one of the poorest countries in the world, producing a shift in total fertility from 7 births per woman to about 5 by the late 1980s, and an continued decline in the early 1990s. With a fertility transition well underway, a second puzzle presents itself: what are convincing explanations of such a decline? Is conventional demographic theory which views fertility decline as the consequence of socio-economic or other structural transformation of society a valid explanation for demographic change in Bangladesh? Or is it more persuasive to view the onset of the fertility transition as a reflection of an ever growing level of poverty in Bangladesh, which compels couples to opt for a smaller number of children? Have the diffusion of new ideas and modernizing trends been responsible? Alternatively, to what extent can demographic change be attributed to the massive investment in resources, policy commitments, and operational measures in the family planning program?

In a recent analysis, Cleland et al. have taken a forceful position on these questions, arguing that the data do not support the conclusion that fertility decline has been driven by socio-economic development, nor that it is predominantly a function of rising levels of poverty. Instead, they conclude that the evidence supporting the influence of the government program is very strong, and suggest that, For Bangladesh the relative importance and primacy of the demand and supply side factors should be reversed. The crucial change that has taken place concerns acceptability of and access to birth control, and not structural change that has driven down the demand for children. While the evidence for a demand-oriented theory of fertility decline in Bangladesh is viewed as weak, the authors nonetheless acknowledge that Bangladesh is affected by changes which, though not amounting to the socio-structural transformations typically associated with fertility decline, may have profound influence. The authors argue:

> Though these changes have not yet brought growing prosperity, their collective impact represents an element of modernization, with unknown but perhaps profound, effects on outlooks and expectations. It is unlikely that family planning would have flourished in the absence of all these changes. Thus the results of our analysis should not be regarded as an emphatic rejection of demand theories of fertility decline. There is simply insufficient evidence, particularly on adult perceptions of the economics of childbearing, to justify such a claim.

In this qualitative analysis of focus group interviews with

women in Matlab on precisely such adult perceptions of not just childbearing but more generally the nature of change within rural society, women's lives in Bangladesh are in transition.

Multiple dimensions of their lives are being transformed, and together these changes explain the interest in family limitation. The presence of a strong program is a major contributing influence in the demographic transition, but social and economic changes, as well as a new mental outlook, new ideas and orientations, also play an important role. The shifts that have taken place are subtle and have not affected everyone equally. They do not amount to a major transformation of economic and social structures, nor to the emergence of entirely new patterns of thought and action. But their influence emerges as a pervasive theme in the many long conversations with rural women of different ages in the Matlab communities as they seek to explain this world and the role of demographic change within it.

The basic argument presented here is very similar to the analysis of Caldwell et al. on the causes of demographic change in south India. The increased economic burden of large families, an increasing influence of a monetized economy as well as critical changes in schooling and the increasing penetration of elements of modern urban life in the village, together with the influence of the program, were seen as the causes of the onset of the fertility transition in south India. Although Bangladesh had not reached the same level of adult literacy as south India, the parallels are important.

Cleland et al. regret the absence of evidence on? people's perceptions regarding the economics of childbearing. Caldwell et al. emphatically affirm the importance of listening to the participants in the process of social change as well, arguing that, "The reasons for this (fertility decline) are known to the participants, and any reported mystery is the product of the nature of large-scale surveys and not of social forces so deep that they are neither noticed nor understood by the actors". Present data from a focus group study with women in the Matlab villages in southern Bangladesh, which suggests that those who participate in the fertility transition are not passive actors in this historic process of change, but are knowledgeable of the multiple changes that affect their lives.

Of course, the Matlab villages do not represent all of Bangladesh, and in that sense the arguments presented here have limitations in explanations of the fertility transition for the country as a whole. Since the eighty villages covered by the Matlab project are in one of the more conservative regions of the country in southern Bangladesh, reachable mainly by river transport, socio-economic change and modernizing influences might be even stronger in other areas. On the other hand, since programmatic influences are unusually strong in Matlab given the special nature of the Matlab MCH-FP project, conclusions presented here are likely to overstate the influence of the program in comparison with other dimensions of change. Limitations also arise from the fact that the data deal with only women's perceptions, and not those of men as well.

A presentation of women's perceptions of changes in contraceptive use and fertility, and then describes the changes they experience in the economic and social circumstances of their lives, including their views of the influence of modernity. Women's reactions to the family planning program as represented by the Matlab community-based family planning worker and by the media. The conclusion draws on insights from the debate on deconstruction in the social sciences in an effort to place the divergent conclusions about the fertility transition in Bangladesh into perspective.

**Transitions in Contraceptive use and Fertility**

In 1988 when data collection for this study was completed, contraceptive prevalence in Matlab had reached 52 percent, with almost half of this prevalence being accounted for by Depo-provera, and the remainder by the pill, sterilization and to a much lesser extent the IUD, condoms, foam, and traditional methods. Since then, prevalence has surpassed 60 percent.

The focus group data show that women are not only aware of widespread contraceptive use in their communities, but they are also aware of the onset of fertility decline. Statements such as the following are common:

> In our mother's period, a mother had 7-8 children. By the grace of the Almighty our development has been made. Nowadays we all use method. They

> (people) have fewer children now. Not more than four.
>
> They (mothers) used to have many children, while we have relatively few. At present the people have 7 or eight children, that is those who do not adopt a method. Many are using family planning methods; users have four to five children. In the past people did not practice family planning and used to have 10-12 children. Nowadays, couples have less children because they use family planning methods more. After three they take operation. People use contraception hence have few children so they are better now.

Associated with this awareness of the changes in contraceptive behavior and fertility is the recognition that the normative context of contraceptive use has been altered. Although norms of shyness and modesty continue to dictate a certain reluctance to address topics of reproductive behavior, especially for young women, participants acknowledge that family planning has become a frequent topic of conversation. While once a subject that could barely be discussed in whispers, there now is an emerging culture of contraception even in remote rural areas of Bangladesh. To use the words of a very young focus group participant - family planning has become like dhal-bhat (rice and pulses), that is like very ordinary or common food. Barriers that existed in the past are beginning to crumble:

> "husbands tell their wives to use family planning even on the night of marriage", or in the past "mothers did not allow their daughters to talk about family planning, now mothers do not object if their daughters learn about family planning."

Women are clear that lower fertility benefits them individually and also benefits their families, but they frequently voice concerns about the dangers of contraceptive use. In fact, they believe that contraceptive use implies a sacrifice which women take upon themselves because of the benefits of lower fertility. They generally do not believe that their spouses should use contraception, because they fear for the well-being of their husbands, upon whose strength and support they depend. Alternatively they argue that men are simply not ready to bear the responsibility of contraceptive use.

We opt for family planning along with problems. It is better than to have a child.

> My husband was also in favor of contraception then I decided, it is better to use method, if there is any side-effect then I might die, which is better than all these botherations.
>
> People ask me what I am doing. I reply that I am taking methods. They express concern of what destruction I am doing to myself by taking family planning methods.
>
> If the women die after taking method, then it is alright, but women cannot go without men.
>
> As I am unable to take any family planning method because of Asthma and am suffering a lot, still my husband will not use anything. I have told him many times but he will not understand.
>
> They (men think that they will lose their work power after vasectomy. They will not be able to work hard. Very few men like to use condom. They do not feel better with condom.

Thus, women are conscious of the fertility transition and the contraceptive revolution that is affecting their communities. As the following part of the demonstrates, they are also aware of broader changes that are affecting their lives in areas that are conventionally considered demand-side determinants of fertility decline.

**Economic and Social Change**

With living standards stagnant and broad indicators of the level of poverty approximately unchanged, Cleland et al. concluded that there has not been a major socio-economic change in Bangladesh that would explain the fertility decline. A slightly different perspective emerges from the analysis of women's perceptions. They do see change in the material and social circumstances of their lives and acknowledge the influence of new ideas. This change is relatively small, by no means amounting to the massive structural transformations that are conventionally associated with a fertility decline. Yet from the perspective of women these changes are full of meaning and significance for reproductive decision-making. The central themes in the focus groups include: the cost of living, the expenses involved in raising children, educational aspirations for children (including daughters), changes in family relations, the dowry system, women's social position, and the influence of modern lifestyles and ideas.

*The cost of living:* The perception of the contraceptive revolution is embedded in a broader consciousness of alterations in people's livelihood and means of survival. Above all women speak about the fact that their families have less land than their parents and attribute this change to population growth, land erosion, or the distress sale of land. In a society where subsistence agriculture is still the dominant means of livelihood, decreased land holding implies food shortages, and many women remember, or at least believe, that resources were more plentiful when their mothers were young. While some families, especially those who can rely on the income from formal wage earners, are perceived to be well off, there is a pervasive sense among the participants that most people cannot keep up with the increases in the cost of living.

> There is less of everything. Lands are getting divided.
>
> Many people are losing land by flood erosion, and the rest is taken for road construction.
>
> Say there were five members in one's house. Those five members gave birth to 10 children. From those 10 children 20 more human beings are born. All these people are now sharing the land property that is being divided among them. The volume of land and property has decreased with the increase of population. Land decreased through fragmentation. When there are 10 sons in a family, land must automatically reduce. Again, if there are too many daughters in a family, parents are obliged to sell portions of their land to meet the expenses of the daughters' marriage.
>
> Things were more in the past, but now we do not get plenty of vegetables and fish due to the population increase.

> There is food problem. Due to excessive rain or flood we are unable to cultivate enough good crops. The land has become subdivided.. The yield of a year is not enough for all the family members.

Given the shortage of land together with the increasing commercialization of the economy and price increases, which are also mentioned as a significant trends, women face increasing problems in providing for their families.

> We have to think twice before eating. If we eat everything in a day, how will we pass other days. Moreover, we have to buy clothes for ourselves and our children, there are educational expenses too.
>
> Nowadays money has less value, while the price of commodities has increased. The more people are earning, the more is their expenditure.
>
> Earlier our parents could buy a bag full of things by selling cow's milk. But now even a person who is earning goes to the market with Taka 300, and he will not be able to fill up this shopping bag with commodities.
>
> Yes, nowadays a bag cannot be filled.
>
> Compared with the past the condition is not good. The cost of good food has increased rapidly. We cannot afford to eat rich food. We live mostly on rice, pulse, or spinach.

Emphatically one woman declared that there was no progress in these communities:

> How could there be development. We lack everything so much that we often become bewildered. Should we give food to our children only or should we wear (clothes) and take food also?

In spite of the many laments about the deterioration of economic conditions, women also realize that some families in the community, namely those able to secure employment, work in contracting or in a variety of other jobs, are better off. The new aspirations for the future of their children, must at least partially be grounded in the recognition of the differential material circumstances that apply to those who begin to participate in the modern sector of the economy, and those who do not.

*The cost of children:* Within an economic context where the conditions of livelihood are perceived to be deteriorating for many members of the community, the cost of raising children is a major concern for women. The conversations revealed that rational calculations about the relationship between food and other supplies, and the number of children in a family are very much part of women's consciousness. For example:

> Those who have fewer children have the advantage of feeding their children better than those who have many.
>
> I need to clean my children with soap which I don't have. How could I then do the job.
>
> If there is one child we can move freely without having any anxiety. People now understand that if there is only one mouth it can be fed by anything, but if there are several mouths, ashes would not be enough to feed them. People have fewer children now. They have less because they can take better care and provide them more with their necessities.
>
> We don't want too many babies because we can't afford to feed them well, or bring them up well.
>
> They know they will not be able to rear their children, will not be able to provide proper food, clothing, education, so they adopt family planning to keep the family small.
>
> We feel that if we have many children our health would break down and we would not be able to build them up as ideal men. So what need of having more children. We will try to educate them, provide them with good clothes, food and will ensure our good health and will be mighty in all respects. But those who do have many children couldn't give them adequate food, clothings and education.

Themes pertaining to the quality of children begin to emerge in the above quotations. It is not enough for children to be fed and clothed; they must be raised to their fullest potential by investing in their future. Evidence presented in subsequent sections of the build further upon these notions, demonstrating that women perceive the raising of children as increasingly costly and thus consider it in their own best interest to have "quality" children.

*Education*: The dominant theme that reverberates throughout all of the focus group transcripts, whether women in their teens, twenties, thirties or forties are talking, is that they see their lives in transition. The world is not what it used to be, stable and predictable. They perceive significant change in the value of education, in the way family members relate to each other, in the financial transactions involved in marriage, and more broadly speaking, in the emergence of a modern lifestyle.

While overall literary and educational levels may not have changed much over the past decade as Cleland et al. indicate, aspirations certainly have. References to the desire for, or interest in, sending children to school appear in relation to many different conversation topics:

> Now people have more interest in education than before. About education everybody's interest is growing.
>
> Now both the guardians and the children themselves have realized the importance of education. So children show their interest thus the guardians become interested and send their children to school.
>
> Parents are putting efforts to make their children educated with their limited resources.
>
> Let us see to what extent Allah helps us.
>
> We didn't take care of the education of our older children. But we have to think of the younger ones. Let us see how Allah helps us.

Education involves expenses even though primary schools are free. Books, appropriate clothing and related educational supplies constitute significant expenditures for many families. While women's aspirations are beginning to focus on the education of their children, they also acknowledge that realizing these hopes may depend on forces beyond their control.

New educational aspirations are associated with related changes in women's approach to the quality of children. Women are not only interested in sending their children to school, they also contrast their approach to child-rearing with that of their mothers:

> We take more care (of children). We try to keep them neat and clean, do not allow them to roam about in the sun. We give them better food and are always forcing them to study. Earlier the mothers did not bother whether the children studied or not. But we are always forcing them to study.
>
> (our mothers) were only busy with husking, boiling of paddy. cooking and other household duties. They used to give birth to many children, but they did not care very much about their children, where they were going or not, what they were eating.

There is interest in the education not only of boys but of girls as well. As is clear from the following comments, the reason for this interest is closely related to the marriage of daughters, to be discussed in greater detail in the subsequent section dealing with the dowry system.

> The value of education is more than before. Even those who eat hand to foot will also send their daughters to school.
>
> Educated daughters can be married off to worthy men and both educated sons and daughters will be able to live better. We also will require less amount of money in their marriage.
>
> Many things have changed. Nowadays people provide education to their children, specially girls. Then they look for an educated and well off groom... While earlier the people used to marry off their daughters to any groom. They never used to see whether he came from a respectable family, whether he was educated or not.

Education is seen as one of the major mechanism for people to attain their vision of a better life. Women argue that:

> The children will lead a better life. And the parent will be proud of them. .... Education has the highest value now. Everyone wants to sit in the upper class. Don't we want to be in upper levels?

(We) will have good days in the future as our children are getting education. The statements just quoted draw a connection between education and a better, more secure future. Women recognize that the future of their children rests with employment in the formal sector of the economy. They understand that education is a major precondition for securing such employment, an investment in the future, not just for men but also for women.

> Our children are being sent to school because it is our duty to educate them. What will happen later, whether they will benefit by education, is left to be seen, because they are now in the process of learning, not bringing income to the house. For example, to begin a business we need capital to invest. Our children are not our capital as yet. We are in the investment stage, providing books, pens and so on without which there can be no education. Life had a different meaning to our forefathers. For them children were a source of income. So, as soon as the children would grow up, they would send them to the field for cultivation work. But now we send them to school on the idea that they would be employed somewhere after their education to earn their livelihood.

*Changes in family relations:* Women in the Matlab communities perceive that family relations are not following the old patterns. The role of parents and parents-in-laws have become weakened, conjugal bonds are stronger, family structures are changing, intergenerational wealth flows are beginning to reverse, and young wives are believed to have a degree of influence that defies tradition. The decreasing role of the mother-in-law, whose position in the traditional extended family was strong is reflected in the following quotes:

> No, they (the mother in laws) do not say anything. All the decisions are made by the husband and the wife. In spite of this will the brides care or listen?.. We used to value our mother-in-law's opinion and decisions. But nowadays the brides do not care. Rather than the mother-in-law has to listen to the brides' order.

Nowadays sons are more inclined to their wives not to the mothers. (women) do not listen to their mothers-in-law or their husbands. It is the husbands who listen to their wives more. Men used to listen to their parents before, but now they act according to their wives demands. They will do whatever their wives say. They will even rebuke their parents for their wives.

> Son's wives say they would not live jointly with their fathers and mothers-in-laws as they say there lacks peace in a joint family.

By contrast, the bond between husband and wife is viewed as strengthened, and couples are "taking liberties" in front of their children that would have been considered shocking in the past. They talk to each other in broad daylight, or discuss family planning:

> Our sons and their wives don't need the nightfall to come. They can talk during the day.
>
> No, they (the young women) never used to talk with their husband about such affairs (when they should have children, how many they should have). The brides used to stay with their mothers and sisters-in-law most of the time. But now we stay near our husbands, take our meal together in front of our parents-in-law.
>
> Nowadays the brides will stay near the husband all day long. They will sit with their husbands holding their neck even in front of the children.
>
> Sons become more selfish and seek their own happiness after marriage. They pay less attention to parents, who have done so much for them. Sometimes the wife forces her husband to quit his parents to avoid their responsibilities and to live happily.
>
> Earlier we used to call our husbands as "Apni" (with honor) but now the girls will address their husbands as "Tumi" (informal you) in front of everyone.

Increased interest in establishing nuclear households was also mentioned. When women explained this change, the new lifestyle theme and the influence of a somewhat diversified economy where some can rely on regular incomes and others not, were mentioned:

> There are too many people. And a single person's

> income cannot serve all. Moreover, the people have become more self-centered. They want to do everything and enjoy the life by themselves. They think that they will not be able to live better if they stay with their parents or brothers.
>
> They (extended families) do not have a congenial relationship. There is lack of love and affection and cooperation. Moreover, there is always some sort of quarrel if there is monetary insolvency and few earning members but many feeding members. That's why they get separated.

Opinions were divided over the issue of whether sons can still be relied upon to support parents in their old age.

If some of these statements, especially those involving the role of women within the family, seem surprisingly strong, it should be remembered that these are conversations in which women compare themselves to standards they feel dominated the lifestyle of an older generation. They may perceive changes in their social life that an outsider would consider extremely small. From a subjective point of view of women who have seen the old ways of life, however, the new patterns may appear genuinely transforming. For them, the old rules have lost some power, though by no means all, and traditional bonds are not as strong as they used to be. With old ties weakening, new ones emerging and, as we will see later on, horizons broadening, the transition in reproductive behavior begins to appear more like a strand in a seamless web of change rather than an isolated phenomenon.

*The dowry system and its effect on women's position:* Changes in marriage transactions from a system of bride prices to dowries are of recent origin in Bangladesh, and have been associated with the forces of modernization and the emergence of the cash economy. A shift towards dowries signifies a deterioration of women's position, rendering them increasingly vulnerable to forces over which they have no control. Concerns about how to procure the resources needed to pay for dowries has assumed the proportions of a financial crisis for families, especially since amounts required to arrange a satisfactory marriage are perceived to be increasing. If parents cannot assemble the required resources for a daughter's marriage, she stays unmarried beyond what villagers consider "marriageable" age, an image that conjures up visions of over-ripe or spoilt fruit. The assets required for dowries lead families to sell land and to incur other heavy financial responsibilities. If parents fail to make contractually established dowry payments, their daughters are likely to be sent back home. Husbands may choose to remarry because they seek another dowry, and women have to submit to the suffering this implies.

While the dowry system with its relentless financial burden has decreased the status of women, its linkage to the cost of childbearing is possibly one of the elements in the new calculus of reproductive choice. For example:

> Nowadays the bridegrooms demand a lot of money, a constructed house, wrist watch, radio, bicycle. The bride's parents are unable to meet such demands and hence are unable to marry off their daughters.
>
> And speaking of girls - daughters - one needs 10 to 12 thousand taka to give a daughter in marriage. This is another reason why people want fewer babies." Everyone cannot afford to spend such a large amount of money. So they have to beg or borrow money from other people.
>
> I also did not have much money. So I borrowed money from others and married off my daughters. I had to spend Taka 50 thousand. So isn't it a great problem for us?.. We have a headache as our daughters are surpassing marriageable age but we are unable to give their hand in marriage.
>
> There was no such problem before... When I got married my in-laws gave me a pair of earrings, a necklace, three saris and they brought sweets and had fun. But now no such thing happens. The parents are afraid if a proposal comes for their daughters. From where will they get so much money? This is our greatest problem. Even greater than food problem.
>
> In the past days there were very much less cost involved in the marriage of girls. So people gave their daughters in marriage easily at the early age. But not the bride groom's party demand one tola of

> gold, a wristwatch, radio, cassette changer, bicycle, cash money etc. as dowry;. They cannot afford these things which causes delay in their daughter's marriage.
>
> Now some people's daughters are engaged in pursuing education. By this time their guardians manage money for the daughter's marriage. So these cases there is delay in their daughter's marriage. They want to ensure good for their daughters by making them educated.

The heavy weight of the dowry in parent's financial calculations was summarized by one woman when she said: "Girls have become a rope around their parents neck". There also is a potential link between the desire for women's education and the dowry system. Educated young women may require less of a dowry, are likely to be considered a more a desirable marriage match by some than uneducated ones, or possibly might be able to earn an income themselves. Thus while there are costs associated with the education of girls, potential advantages are perceived as well. Certainly, considerations of the future price of marriage of daughters are likely to have assumed a compelling influence in planning family size.

*Women's emerging sense of self-esteem and freedom:* While the increased payments and expectations of the dowry system signify a deterioration in women's status, their consciousness appears to be moving in a direction of greater strength. In fact, one of the surprises in these data is women's emerging sense of themselves as worthy individuals capable of thinking and acting independently, and deserving to enjoy at least some of the pleasures of modern life. Such self-esteem is not what one expects in a culture that extols women's honor but traditionally deprives them of a sense of personal efficacy. That old patterns are changing is clear from many points in the conversations:

> No woman used to go out from the house before. As the country has obtained independence, so they (women) have become independent too.
>
> I was married in the month of Bhadra and the country obtained independence(check) in the month of charia. Since then the women have become

> independent.
>
> Yes, (women are) very much independent. They are receiving more education and are willing and fit to earn their own living.
>
> There has been lots of improvement.... The women are getting educated and are able to work. We are able to earn money, mix with different people; we are freer than before are able to move around the village.
>
> We also encourage our daughters to get educated so that they will be able to get a job and earn for maintaining a better life. These were not before. The girls were kept under the veil, they were not allowed to do anything.

Women are also aware that some of these changes involve underlying tensions and disapproval from men. For example one woman commented, "My husband gets annoyed quite often. He says that when I come from the bazaar, I see many young girls about 19 or 20 years of age walking along the road, staring at the people and sometimes laughing." According to the norms of the traditional society, women (let alone young ones) are not to be seen in public places unless they are covered by a burkah. For men who have been socialized within a culture that dictates women's honor must be protected by hiding them from public gaze, the sight of young women who freely examine the world around them is shocking. The focus group participant went on to explain: "No woman used to go out from the house, specially to the bazaar, before.

In fact the men used to buy all the essential commodities. But now they go to the market themselves if they want a small thing." While contraceptive use is at times viewed as a sacrifice, it is also an important ingredient in women's new freedom. In explaining why women tend to be more interested in family planning than men, for example, one woman pointed out that "women have become very much concerned about themselves. They want to live in peace and happiness, as they suffer maximum." Women in rural Bangladesh work extremely hard, and they are the ones who bear the burden of raising many children.

With contraception available and with the concomitant emergence of the idea that women have a right to be concerned about their own well-being and not only about that of others, the benefits of contraceptive use are beginning to be apparent. They will have more time and energy to develop a closer bond with their husband, and to take better care of their health. The connection to their health condition is also clear from the frequent comment that "women's health condition deteriorates if they have frequent births." There is agreement among the younger and the older focus group participants that the younger women are even freer than those who are over thirty. The freedom to delay the onset of childbearing is a central element in this transition. As one of the older women put it:

> Nowadays all are very conscious(about family planning). Especially the girls. They want to remain young and pretty. So they tell their husbands on the night of marriage that they do not want many children. The husbands also agree as they too want their wives to remain young and their breasts to remain pointed. But we did not say such a thing to our husbands. We were shy to talk about this. That's why we have as many children as our husbands wanted.

Though significant, the emerging sense of self-esteem and freedom experienced especially by the younger women, does not imply substantial undermining of the institution of patriarchy. Women continue to depend in large measure upon the presence and support of their husbands or their sons. Earlier comments about women's reluctance to see men use contraception serve as examples of this continued dependence.

*Modernization:* Women not only see their own lives in transition, they perceive the world around them to be in a process of change to which they attach the label of modernity. New modes of transport, electricity, and the media have reached the villages, more schools are being built, and more markets exist than in the past. Exposure to a world beyond the boundaries of traditional rural communities brings new ideas, including signs of the orientations and values of a commercialized, consumer society.

> Yesterday, a motor-cycle was going by. My daughter came running to fetch me in order to see the motor-cycle. My daughter is now seeing this and I myself also saw it. But did my mother see such a thing before? It's new in the village. Changes are taking place day by day.
>
> Earlier we did not have any electricity, but now there has been electricity supply in the village. Almost each and every bari has electricity. There are hospitals and small clinics in different places. Hence we get treatment facilities There were very few schools and colleges before. But now there are lots of schools and colleges. There are also more weekly markets and bazaars.
>
> The people before were satisfied with only one cloth. All the family members could use a single pair of shoes in turn.
>
> Nowadays the people wear clothes in competition. If another person has five saris I will require eight saris. We require three, four pairs of shoes. Before the people used to walk barefoot, or used to wear sandals made of wood. Before seven brothers would share one shirt. But now there is competition among brothers as well. If a brother has a new shirt another one will try to make two shirts. They will not even allow each other to wear each other's clothes.
>
> Education has increased and all are modern. Everything has changed. Boys and girls are growing up together.
>
> The generations are changing. Time are also changing. People now want to be modern, they want to live up to date. They want to live and eat well.

People are beginning to wear clothes in competition and expect more for their lives than the bare minimum essentials for survival. In wanting to live up to date and be modern, younger women contrast their own expectations with those of their mothers. A self-congratulatory sense of superiority pervades some of the remarks:

> They were aloof from all other fancies. Only they thought of paddy and eating. But nowadays

> whether we eat properly or not we want to spend some money on fancies. We want beautiful saris and ornaments, cosmetics. Listen Apa, we can easily follow what program or song is being played in a radio or how a Lux soap differs from a Lifeboy but our mothers are quite blank in this regard.
>
> Mothers cannot wash the body without a Bangla soap, but we use Lux, Cosco, Gacotus, Lemondew. They do not know the names even.
>
> We know about different types of bangles and request husbands to bring those, but old people say only about rubber bangles. As we have seen all these in our days so we can say about this.
>
> We can ask for organdi sari, but they are happy with this simple and ordinary sari.

An older woman laughingly comments on the difference in her lifestyle and that of her daughters and daughters-in-law: "My mother was simple like me. She was not modern and with the times. (Daughters)wear different saris. The girls and the daughter-in-laws wear alike. Sometimes, we also wear them, when they offer us." Almost sounding like the mother of a teenage daughter in an industrialized society, another older participant acknowledges that women have to purchase the newly available consumer goods for their daughters, and allow them to depart from the traditional dress-code for women:

> You see, in our times we never used Snow (a cream) and powder, but we have to buy these for our girls. This is a must for them. In our times we wore only saris, but they wear Shalwar-kameez (trousers and long shirt). We have to buy them the things that are available these days.

Having fewer children is viewed as an integral part of the view of a better and more comfortable life:

> They (the women) have taken family planning methods for their own happiness and peace. They want to live better, so that they do not have any trouble getting food and beautiful clothes.
>
> We are better off, because you know Apa, we were eight brothers and sisters. My mothers was lean and weak. I never saw her in good health. She had no

time to take rest. She spent the whole day in cooking and washing. But I am free from all such sort of botheration. I have only three children. I am able to take rest, look after my children properly.

Women have begun to focus on their own well-being and are trying to escape from what some perceive as the drudgery that characterized the life of their mothers. Their horizons are expanding. Women are better off because, as one of them put it, "now they are more exposed and get to hear many things. They watch, they get to know." Women want to be part of the commercial culture that is emerging around them. Within these aspirations many children are viewed as "botheration".

**The Role of the Family Planning Programme**

In the Matlab villages women are exposed to two programmatic influences - those of the government family planning program, which reaches them predominantly through the media, and through the special Matlab MCH-FP program, which affects their lives primarily through the community-based family planning worker. Both of these constitute significant innovations in women's lives, although the influence of the worker is likely stronger than that of the media. The presence of the Matlab MCH and family planning project has been a major influence in the lives of local women. Just as in the government family planning program, the link to rural women is a community-based family planning worker, who visits women on a regular basis. In contrast to the public sector program, however, the scope and intensity of contacts between the worker and community women differ considerably. Contact is bi-weekly, and contraceptive and maternal and child health services are real and have been sustained over time. The influence of the community-based family planning worker on women's lives is multifaceted, transcending in several respects conventional notions of the functions of "systems of supply".

*A trusted friend:* The transition of the community's opinion about the Matlab community based family planning worker. Initially portrayed as a "devil woman" who had come to the villages to destroy the community's well-being, the worker succeeded in gaining acceptance for her professional role, established herself as a social leader and maintained her honor as a woman. One quote may suffice to characterize the transition to her role within the community:

> People said, she will kill all the women by feeding them those medicines. Women used to hide themselves, on seeing Mahamuda (the worker) coming to her house. Mahamuda spent her whole day explaining and making the women easy to talk to her. After her continuous saying and seeing her day after day, she became famous to the women.

There are difference in the performance of individual workers and not all of them are necessarily equally appreciated; one was widely disliked for her arrogant personality and lack of support to women when they felt they needed her. Nonetheless, most are so highly respected by both women and their husbands that in one of the focus groups, women commented in response to the moderator's questions whether they considered the worker a relative:

> Woman 1: We think of her as more than a relative.
>
> Woman 2: Her feeling for us, her behavior towards us, concern for us are much more pleasant than (that of) a relative.
>
> Similarly:
>
> Women l: She has become so close that she is more than our sister.
>
> Woman 2: We do not feel better if we do not see her for one or two days. We wish that she was able to visit us every day. We like to chat with her.

Overcoming the fear of contraception: A recurrent theme in comments on the worker's role is the reassurance she provides to community women about contraceptive methods, and about that fact that she will assist women if they experience any difficulties. As one woman put it: "She is able to overcome fear about methods. That's why so many women are taking family planning methods. Otherwise many women would not have taken family planning methods." If a worker does not perform this function, as was true in one case, she was heavily criticized with several negative comments about her failure to assist women with side-effects.

*Overcoming the opposition of family members:* When women opt to use contraception without informing their families, the worker is frequently called upon to mediate when others discover it. "She explains the benefit of family planning methods to the husbands and mother-in-law and makes them understand why the woman is using a method".

*Providing access to the means of contraception:* Women in Matlab are well aware of the fact that the family planning worker distributes contraceptives, provides contraceptive injections, and facilitates access to clinic-based methods. For example, "If anyone wants to get sterilized, then Rekha (the worker) makes all the arrangements. She goes to the Matlab Centre and fixes the schedule. Then she makes arrangements for the boat. Takes the client with her. Stays there during the operation and afterwards and then brings her home."

*The thinkability of reproductive decisions:* Coale argued that one of the preconditions for fertility decline is that reproductive decisions must be perceived to fall within the calculus of rational choice. Van de Walle expanded on this idea to point out that "numeracy about children". Historically, thinking about children in numerical terms became part of people's mental outlook as they passed through a process of reproductive change. Some of the comments from community women speak to these issues quite explicitly. For example, one woman commented that people who have adopted contraception have four children, but those who don't "have no measuring rod". Others also confirm the notion that previously the very concept of family limitation did not exist, and that the worker had a major part in introducing it. For example in response to questions about why people want fewer children, or about the role of the worker, women said:

> It is due to the family planning program. If this program had not been introduced no one would have reduced fertility. The people used to beg food and stay ill fed before. Still they wanted many children. Was there any such force before, as they are now saying "two are enough?". They used to say "God will give as many as he wishes. We have no hand over his desires".
>
> We see Mahamuda here with family planning methods. She taught us at the same time that God has given us the strength to decide about birth control.

> For the first time Momtaz had given us a clear concept of family planning. As she is our close person, and as she is a most reliable one, and as she is giving us continuous help, we decided to take family planning.

This, as well as the earlier comment that those who do not control their fertility "have no measuring rod", affirm how clearly participants in the fertility transition perceive the changes that are transforming their lives, and how strong a role the worker plays in these changes. The above comments also suggest a strong influence over family size preferences, a topic that will be addressed in greater detail below.

*Influencing family size preferences:* While many focus group participants credit the worker with convincing women to use family planning, it is not always easy to disentangle whether they are referring to the provision of the information and means, the communication of the thinkability of reproductive choice, the creation of demand for methods by overcoming fear or family opposition, or to her influence in readjusting family size preference. However, some comments address the issue quite directly while also acknowledging the complexity of the issue. For example, when the moderator asked whether the worker can stop those who want more children from having another birth, women answered that this depends on the situation and that the worker cannot force anyone. Finally one woman asserted: "We have restricted our family size and other women also were convinced by the persuasion of M. and are restricting their family size."

Other comments also support a strong influence of the worker and the program:

> People are observing that, by having few children, they are now enjoying a happy family life in which the working of CHW (the worker) has great contribution. They realize that such comfort would have not been possible if they had many children.
>
> (People have fewer children) because the government is telling them to have few children. They are imposing this on the people. Otherwise would people want to reduce fertility forcingly?
>
> They are taking family planning methods after

> listening to the speeches from time to time.
>
> Debi goes from village to village and explains that too many children is a problem for mothers. The women have begun to understand.

However, in the same sessions a woman also affirms the autonomy of reproductive decision-making: "It struck our mind that if we take many children, how could we give them education, dress them up." The simultaneous influence of the compelling social circumstances and of the worker are well represented in the passage which followed the above comment:

> Moderator: Who taught you these ideas?
>
> Woman 1 : Automatically such idea came in our mind.
>
> Woman 2. : By persistently hearing about family planning and its advantages, women's consciousness has been shaped.
>
> Woman 3: We became convinced that family planning would ensure well-being for us.

The relationship between the social and economic factors that create demand for family limitation and the worker's role in providing access to methods was lucidly summarized:

> One needs 10 to 20 thousand taka to give one's daughter in marriage. This too is a problem. It causes one a lot of worries, which tell upon one's health. Under the circumstances, one has to use one of the birth-control methods advised by "the doctor". There are too many mouths to feed. so one has no choice but to go for a birth-control method. Some choose injectables, some prefer copper-T, some condoms. some people think that injectables are quite good. Others however complain of their side-effects. Nevertheless, they continue to use that method as the need to limit family size is urgent.

*The worker as social leader, modernizing influence and role model:* The influence of the Matlab worker by far exceeds her formally defined family planning and health functions. She mediates conflicts in the community, especially conflicts between husbands and wives, advises women on marriage arrangements, and is consulted in financial transactions. She makes a wide range of suggestions to women about how they should lead their lives. And women generally acknowledge her enlightening influence, though not always as vividly as in the following remark:

> She gave us the idea about many things. She said that "Bhabi, this is good and that is bad. You should act accordingly". You see if a dirty pot is rubbed with ash every day, it will become clean. So like this she also came from time to time and explained everything. Thus helped to remove the black dirt from our mind it turned white. Gradually we came to like her. She helps us a lot.

The imagery of black dirt being removed from women's minds suggests that women themselves perceive they are exposed to new ideas and influences. Not only does the worker provide access to contraception, she provides a link to modern trends and ideas. She is an agent of the Matlab family planning project, but also of forces of modernity and change, in which the role of woman remains less restricted and confined than in the past. In a social and cultural context where women are traditionally sheltered from outside influences, the significance of her contribution to the lives of local women is powerful. In the words of one of the participants: "She is the one who has helped women become more conscious about themselves." Many view her as a role model they wish they could emulate, or that suggests a path that the daughters might be able to pursue:

> We ourselves feel that had we been educated like Bethar Maa, we too could have worked outside the home and earned money. Unfortunately, we don't have any education.
>
> If any of their daughters don't want to go to school, her parents persuade her by telling her that by learning she will be able to wear saree like Mahmuda and could be able to practice as a doctor and earn money.

*The influence of the media:* Just as the worker represents two influences, the media also have dual effects on women. Availability of radios had become widespread in the Matlab villages at the time the focus group sessions were conducted. Women consistently report that they are aware of the radio programs on family planning and acknowledge their influence, although frequently this influence occurs in conjunction with the interpersonal exchange with the worker.

We heard many things on the family planning program but did not believe in them. We came to understand more and believed it after M. explained everything clearly to us.

In the past we heard about methods but did not believe. But now we listen to the radio and Mahmuda comes to us and explained about methods, we understood the family planning methods. Mainly Mahmuda's visit made the people aware of contraceptives. Initially we refused Mahamuda but after her repeated motivation people understood.

By continuous persuasion of M. and by regular listening to the radio's family planning program our desire for contraception got the shape.

> Husband used to listen to the radio program on family planning where people are asked to take family planning. Everyone is listening to the radio program and what is said in it. After listening to the radio he asked to take family planning.

Women's perceptions of how their lives are changing through a textual analysis of focus group data conducted with women in the Matlab community. The central dimensions of this change consist of the new culture of contraception, increases in the costs of living and raising families, rising educational aspirations, changes in family relations and in women's social position and sense of freedom, the growing influence of modernization, as well as of the presence of a strong program whose key elements are the media and the community-based family planning worker. In analyzing these changes found myself increasingly skeptical of the major conclusion drawn by Cleland et al.in their study of fertility decline in Bangladesh. Their conclusion that Bangladesh "appears to possess no features that are conducive to fertility decline except for a strong, persistent government commitment to reducing population growth" simply does not fit the picture that emerges from the data. Significance of the supply-side factors in explaining the fertility transition in Bangladesh. The data from this study support the conclusion that a very strong programmatic influence as represented both by the media and especially by the Matlab community-based family planning worker exists. The influence of the supply-side is particularly strong in Matlab, but the evidence of a programmatic effect in other parts of the country is persuasive as well.

Have the villages served by the Matlab project become so thoroughly transformed by the activities of the research staff and special project activities that Matlab women's perceptions have no relevance for the remainder of Bangladesh? Such effects cannot be completely brushed aside. Exposure to outside influences represented by researchers, including foreigners, and other project staff has been considerable and has undoubtedly enhanced the modernizing trends that exist elsewhere as well as contributed to an enhanced resource base through the creation of project generated employment. But to argue that these account for even a substantial portion of women's perceptions of change in their lives appears excessive. More likely than not, the lessons from Matlab about the occurrence of social and economic change have significance for the country as a whole, just as earlier Matlab had significance in demonstrating the potential for programmatic effects.

However, incremental change in several important spheres of women's lives can be clearly seen in the data presented here. Some of these were also noted by Cleland et al., for example, the increasing fragmentation of land holdings, and increased schooling, although the authors do not attribute any significance to these in their overall conclusion. The point here is that what appear to be small changes as measured by objective indicators, are not necessarily so small or insignificant in terms of the actual life experience of people.

Deconstructionist theory in the social sciences provides a useful perspective on the type of disagreements that the experience of Bangladesh has elicited over time, and to which this contributes. Deconstructionist theory argues that there can be no stable or lasting principle, theories or doctrines. Instead knowledge is always in a process of being constructed, then taken apart by critical analysis (deconstructionism) and eventually reconstituted (reconstructed) into new intellectual frameworks. Without wanting to sound too presumptuous, suggest that the dialogue on fertility and its decline in Bangladesh can be understood within the logic of such a deconstructionist process. Theory construction over questions of the potential for fertility decline in Bangladesh began with statements about the primacy of demand, as illustrated most prominently in the writings of Cain and Demeney who saw evidence of strong socio-economic and cultural supports for high fertility norms with little potential for a supply-side role. With a fertility decline well underway, Cleland et al. inherently "deconstruct" arguments about the primacy of demand in order to do justice to the important contribution of the forces of supply. In making this valuable contribution to our understanding, the authors nonetheless continue to reinforce an unhelpful theoretical stance in the population field. That theoretical stance consists of a tendency oriented towards mutually exclusive supply-versus-demand explanations of fertility decline, and the concomitant premise that demand-side determinants must be of major proportions in order to exert an influence.

An appropriate "reconstruction" of the evidence for Bangladesh suggests the simultaneous effect of both demand and supply. It further suggests that in the presence of strong systems of supply, relatively small or incremental change in socio-economic conditions or modernizing influences may produce a significant fertility decline. A strong program magnifies demand-side effects by helping people understand that the world around them is changing, and to interpret such change in the context of decisions about family size and the use of contraception. The reconstructionist approach suggested here in no sense undermines the importance of supply-side determinants. However, by emphasizing both supply and demand it takes a different reading on some of the data presented by Cleland et al., interpreting them in light of the qualitative evidence of women's perceptions of the changes in their lives. As pointed out above, Cleland et al. discard the evidence of shrinking farm size and increased schooling in their conclusion. Listening to women's voices and interpreting them in light of theory that allows for the simultaneous and interactive effects of supply and demand suggests a different conclusion. Shrinkage in farm size, and increased schooling may be small, but in conjunction with strong program influence and other modernizing influences in the economy and the society, these contribute toward the creation of a new calculus of reproductive choice that lends support to smaller families, and to the use of modern contraception.

# 7

# Women in Politics

## Rights to Political Participation

The Constitution of Bangladesh provides equal opportunities for women to participate in politics and public life and it is in the unique situation of having women in the posts of both Prime Minister and Leader of the Opposition. Furthermore Bangladesh is in the even more unique position in having two women Prime Ministers succeeding each other. Women as voters are gaining in visibility and political strength. The turnout of women in the 1996 Parliamentary Elections was phenomenal.

Parliament: There are 30 reserved seats for women in the Parliament to ensure their participation in politics in addition to the 300 elected seats. Although women are equally eligible to contest the elected seats, very few women have been elected to the Parliament through direct electoral process. However, women's participation is gradually increasing. While only 5 parties put up 15 candidates in 1986, in 1991 16 parties put up 40 candidates. In 1996, 36 women candidates were nominated. From these 5 women won 11 seats. In the by-elections held on 5 September 1996, two more women were elected, bringing the number of directly elected women to seven.

In the present Cabinet four of the twenty-four ministers are women (including the Prime Minister). They have been given the posts of Agriculture/Water Resources/Relief , Environment and Forestry and State Minister for Education.

Local Government: Women's participation in local government is another arena of political participation. Women have reserved seats in all municipal and local government bodies. Rural Local Government is a two-tier system with

Union Parishads (Councils) and Zila Parishads (District Councils). There are 4,434 Union Parishads and 64 Zila Parishads. Local Bodies in the urban areas include 4 city corporations and 119 Municipalities. Three seats are reserved for women in all of these. Formerly women were nominated to these seats. Since 1992 they are selected on the basis of indirect election by the other directly elected members. In the Union Council elections women have started to contest the elected seats with increasing success. In the 1988 elections 79 women contested the elections in 4401 Unions and 1 was elected Chairperson. In 1992, 115 contested the elections in 4,443 Unions and 15 were elected Chairpersons. The next Union Parishad elections are due in 1997.

In the 1994 City Corporation election 17 women contested but none won. In 1996 two women were elected directly. The next municipal elections are due in 1998 and City Corporation elections are due in 1999.

Despite some improvements womenþs participation in the political process remains very marginal. The reasons for this are varied and include lack of appropriate and adequate organizational arrangements within political parties for womenþs participation, low participation of women in the political parties, low women's participation in the decision making bodies of the political parties, lack of political discourse on women's issues within political parties, lack of political training for women, the constraints of the present political culture which include the use of muscle men, violence, "black money", etc.

**Reservation of Seats**

However, the reservation of seats for women in elected bodies is having a positive impact in that it is ensuring a minimum of womenþs representation and it is enabling women to learn about the workings of the different bodies and the political process. Women as voters are also increasingly exercising their rights and becoming more aware of the implications and dimensions of the political process. Observations have shown that women's participation as voters has also increased although precise figures are not available. The June 1996 Parliament elections saw a phenomenal turnout of women.

**Women in Public Service**

The Government has also taken special measures to ensure the presence of women in the Government, for the formulation of public policy and the implementation thereof and to hold public office and perform public functions at all levels of Government.

Since 1982 women have been regularly appearing at public service examinations and are being recruited into the regular cadre services. In order to increase the number of women in the administration a quota system was introduced for women, which is applicable for all types of public appointment. Under this arrangement 10 percent of recruitment to gazetted posts and 15 percent of recruitment to non-gazetted posts are reserved for women. There is also a provision for reserving 60 percent of recruitment of primary school teachers for women.

In addition a special initiative has recently been taken to appoint women to senior levels i.e. Deputy Secretary and Joint Secretary posts.

**Civil Service**

In one of the recent recruitments to the Bangladesh Civil Service (15th examinations, 1993/94) out of a total of 1144 available posts 858 were filled. According to the application of the reserved quota for women 114 posts were reserved for them of which only 67 were filled. In addition 70 women out of a total of 417 were recruited through the merit quota and 26 women out of a total of 368 were recruited through the district quota. In all 163 women i.e. 19 percent of total recruitment were recruited through various quotas.

In a recent recruitment to the Education Cadre (16th examinations, 1993/94) out of a total of 1373 posts available 1348 were filled of which 407 (30 percent) were women. Out of 137 posts reserved for women under the "women's quota" 112 were filled. The rest of the women were recruited under the merit quota (166/618) and the district quotas (129/617) (18).

Recent experience shows that although women's reserved quotas are not being fulfilled the percentage of women actually recruited is higher 19 percent and 30 percent as mentioned above. At present women constitute 7 percent of gazetted officers and 7.4 percent of other posts. The impact of the quotas are, however, negligible as very few new posts are available. There is very little impact at senior levels.

The worst performers in terms of fulfillment of the womenþs quota have been the public sector corporations where only 5 percent of staff are women. One reason for the poor performance of the autonomous bodies may be that a large number of public sector corporations have mills and factories under their authority where the number of women is very low.

**Women's Participation in Non-government Organizations**

Another arena of womenþs participation in public life is through non-government organizations. There are at present more than 1200 women's organizations registered with the Department of Women's Affairs. These provide a means of women's participation in public life. Various organizations are consulted by the Government for policy making or involved in collaborative programmes through the BJMS and the field offices of the Department of Womenþs Affairs.

There is a strong and active womenþs movement from grassroots to national level which is playing an active role in demanding legal and policy reforms, in mobilizing women to avail of services and facilities available and in changing cultural and social stereotypes about women.

**Equal Opportunity for International Representation and Participation**

State Parties shall take all appropriate measures to ensure to women, on equal terms with men and without any discrimination, the opportunity to represent their Governments at the international levels and to participate in the work of international organizations.

Although women have the right to represent the Government internationally, in reality women's representation has been virtually nil. The need for the representation of women in national and international arenas is recognized. There are only 14 women in the diplomatic service and there has been only one woman ambassador in 1980 and one at present. Various delegations have included women. There are also a number of women serving in various international and UN organizations abroad. However no statistics can be provided.

Of note is that the present Chair of the CEDAW Committee is a Bangladeshi woman and there is a Bangladeshi Resident Representative in the United Nations Development Programme.

**Equal Rights with Regard to Nationality**

1. State Parties shall grant women equal rights with women to acquire, change or retain their nationality. They shall ensure in particular that neither marriage to an alien or change of nationality by the husband during marriage shall automatically change the nationality of the wife, render her stateless or force upon her the nationality of the husband.
2. State Parties shall grant women equal rights with men with respect to the nationality of their children.

Nationality in Bangladesh is determined by birth. Although no reservation has been made to this article of the Convention the Bangladeshi Citizenship Act is discriminatory. Women have equal rights with men to acquire, change or retain their nationality.

They can obtain passports without the signatures of their husbands or fathers. However they do not have equal rights with respect to the nationality of their children. According to Citizenship Act of 1951, citizenship can be transmitted from the father to his children but not from the mother. Also a woman's husband cannot be entitled to citizenship through her. The spouse of a Bangladeshi man may receive citizenship but the contrary is not true.

Measures are being taken by Government to ensure equality between men and women with regard to citizenship rights. In fact the laws in this area are part of the colonial legacy and have not recently been reviewed or revised.

**Equal Rights in the Field of Education**

State parties shall take all appropriate measures to eliminate discrimination against women in order to ensure to them equal rights with men in the fields of education and in particular to ensure on a basis of equality of men and women.

a) The same conditions for career and vocational guidance for the achievement of diplomas in educational establishments of all categories in rural as well as in urban areas; this equality shall be ensured in pre-schools, general, professional and higher technical education, as well as in all types of vocational training;

b) Access to the same curricula; the same examinations; teaching staff with qualifications of the same standard and school premises and equipments of same quality;

c) The elimination of any stereotyped roles of men and women at all levels and in all forms of education by encouraging co-education and other types of education which will help to achieve this aim and, in particular, by the revision of textbooks and school programmes and the adaptation of teaching methods;

d) The same opportunities to benefit from scholarships and other study grants;

e) The same opportunities for access to programmes of continuing education , including adult and functional literacy programmes, particularly those aimed at reducing, at the earliest possible time, any gap in education existing between men and women;

f) The reduction of female dropout rates and the organization of programmes for girls and women who have left school prematurely;

g) The same opportunities to participate actively in sports and physical education

h) Access to specific educational information to help ensure health and well-being of families, including information and advice on family planning.

Policies: The Constitution of Bangladesh provides for the Government to adopt effective measures to establish a uniform, mass oriented and universal system of education and to extend free and compulsory education to all children.

Universalization of primary education and eradication of illiteracy are priorities for the Government.. To ensure education for all and eradicate illiteracy a division called Primary and Mass Education Division was created in 1992 and placed under the Prime Minister. Primary education has been made compulsory by the Primary Education Compulsory Act of 1990.

Considering the high level of illiteracy, the Fourth Five Year Plan incorporated the objectives of universal primary education and non formal primary education to reduce mass illiteracy. The allocation for education sector expenditure was increased in the Plan. The whole country was to be covered in a phased manner by the year 2000 under the universal primary education programme.

The National Plan of Action on Education (1991-2000) sets the following targets:

* raising the gross enrolment rate at the primary level from 76 percent to 95 percent
* raising girl's gross enrolment rate at the primary level to 94 percent
* raising the completion rate at the primary level from 40 percent to 70 percent
* raising adult literacy rate from 35 percent to 62 percent
* increasing female literacy rate from 24 percent to 50 percent by 2000

The National Plan of Action includes the elimination of gender disparity; expansion of non- formal education and undertaking of social mobilization programmes.

The Draft Participatory Perspective Plan (1995-2010) has set the following objectives and targets:

* ensuring enhanced participation of women at all levels of education
* continuing and expanding the free tuition and stipend programme for secondary girls students;
* increasing enrolment of secondary students, particularly girls;
* accelerating the expansion of facilities for women's education to reduce the educational gap between the sexes.

**Division of Subjects**

In school and at higher levels women are allowed to take the same subjects as boys. Same curriculum and examination procedures are followed for both boys and girls. Scholarships at various levels (primary, secondary, SSC, HSC and University) are given on the basis of merit and girls/women have equal access to these provisions. Since fewer women than men go into higher education, it is mostly boys/young men who derive the benefits of such government provisions. Provisions have been made to recruit women teachers to sixty percent of the vacant positions in primary schools. An effort has been made to recruit 7000 women teachers for secondary schools i.e at least 2 women teachers in each school. These teachers will also be given a year's training with a stipend prior to their appointment. Accommodation facilities will also be provided for women recruits after their appointment.

The allocation for education sector has increased to 16 percent of the total public sector expenditure in 1994-95 from 11 percent in 1991-92. This is the highest allocation in the budget for any one sector. The government provides 80 percent of the teacher's salary of the registered private schools. A target has been set to establish at least one separate girls' secondary school in each thana.

**Secondary Education**

To reduce the disparity in access to secondary schools between boys and girls, special provisions have been made which include:

a) A nation wide female stipend programme at the secondary level, to support girls in grades 6-10 studying in recognized institutions (schools/madrassas) outside metropolitan areas. They receive a stipend for books and are provided free tuition against a payment to the school by the government. The objectives are to retain female students at the secondary stage and thereby promote higher education; increase the enrolment rates and reduce dropout rates and also control population growth rate by discouraging girls from marrying before 18 years of age.

b) Providing salaries for additional secondary teachers required for the increased enrolment: The number of secondary schools has increased from 8137 in 1990 to 9352 in 1994 (about 15 percent). This has reduced the distances children have to travel to reach schools, an important factor for the expansion of girls' education.

c) Occupational skill training for secondary school girls: Girls leaving formal schooling (at least at grade 8) are assisted to acquire skills suitable for wage employment or self employment on a pilot basis.

d) Public awareness programme for the education of girls: Media campaigns have been launched for promoting girls' education through various means. These include TV spots, radio programme and a special project called "Meena" for the promotion of the rights of the girl child.

e) Water supply and sanitation programme for girls: Support will be given for hygiene education, latrine construction and rehabilitation, and the sinking of tubewells. At present, only 28 percent of the total state owned schools have separate toilets for girls.

f) A Food for Education programme has been undertaken to increase enrolment and reduce dropout rates. Students are given food in the form of wheat on a monthly basis attending school regularly. A study has found attendance has increased by 14.7 percent and drop out decreased by 7.6 percent.

g) Secondary education upto grade X outside municipal areas has been made free.

h) A girl child who is the only child of parents residing outside municipal area is given the opportunity to study upto degree level free of cost.

The Government has recently decided to make Higher Secondary Education for girls free as well. Steps are underway in this regard.

Women's participation in technical education has traditionally been insignificant. The total number of girls in the Vocational Training Institutes (VTI) in the country was 69 in 1990 and reached 191 in 1994. There is one women's polytechnic institute and the number of students in all polytechnic including this one was 655 in 1994.

In the private sector, a medical college has been established exclusively for girls. Some colleges have been upgraded as universities. A number of other private universities and medical colleges have been established and girls are equally qualified for admission. However, in many cases girls cannot access these institutions as the expenses involved may be prohibitive. Among adolescents, a large proportion has never attended schools. The Directorate of Non-Formal Education aims to cover 300,000 adolescent girls and boys during 1992-96. The role of NGO's in enhancing female education has been recognized and emphasized by the government. NGOs like the Bangladesh Rural Advancement

Committee (BRAC), Gono Shahajja Sangstha (GSS), Proshika, Saptagram Nari Swanirvar Parishad and Community Development Centre (CODEC) and Friends in Village Development in Bangladesh (FIVDB) are playing a vital role in providing non-formal education to children and adults in the country.

Many of the organizations have designed their own models of gender sensitive functional literacy programmes. BRAC has established over 36,000 non-formal schools in rural Bangladesh with 1.3 million students and atleast 70 percent of the students in each school are supposed to be girls.

Since the state is not in a position to ensure primary education for all due to various resource constraints it has to depend on parental motivation and attitudes to achieve this. Since no fines or penalties are imposed on the guardians for non-compliance, parents may chose not to send their daughters to school. Free education in most cases means only free tuition and for higher level education other factors such as clothing, books, fees for school/college final examination and security on the way to school often affect girls'/women's participation. The concentration of higher educational institutions in the urban areas often prevents girls in rural areas from continuing with their studies as parents often do not have the resources to send their daughters to urban areas and worry about the lack of secure residential facilities for girls near the educational institutions. A large percentage of the dropouts and some of those who have actually completed primary education remain functionally illiterate as adequate measures are not taken to retain literacy.

The number of female teacher is a factor influencing girls' enrolment rates at primary and secondary levels of education.

The number of female teachers as well as the number of women in education management i.e. in the decision making positions in the different directorates under the Ministry of Education is very low and not enough to influence decisions. Since new recruitment is limited, only 27 percent of all teachers are female.

Continuation of positive discrimination in recruitment for a long period will be necessary to reach equality. Contrary to the provision stating that the same curricula should be followed by both sexes a few subjects are specific for girls or boys.

At a higher level women can study agriculture but cannot study marine engineering as such institutions do not have facilities to accommodate women. Women lack information about the existing options, the facilities available to accommodate women are often inadequate and the perceived gender role and division of labour influences the selection of subjects for girls and boys. In the engineering field, more women enter into architecture and civil engineering than into other options.

Vocational counselling for guidance on careers is generally not available and it is absent for girls. Social norms also limit the scope for girls to pursue careers even after having obtained the necessary qualifications. Curricula are not gender sensitive and often reflect the traditional roles of men and women, thereby reinforcing them. Teachers training curricula also do not take into account women's multiple responsibilities. The existence of various methods and systems of education, such as madrassa education, may be an obstacle to a more uniform gender sensitive curriculum being promoted.

# 8

# The Assessment

Bangladesh is one of the seven countries in the world where the number of men exceeds the number of women. According to various indicators the status of women in Bangladesh is much lower than that of men. The cultural and social religious values and practices have reinforced the lower status of women accorded to them in society and have limited their opportunities for education, technical and vocational training, employment and participation in the overall development process. Socio-economic changes triggered by increasing rates of landlessness and impoverishment have had a profound impact on women's lives. Greater numbers of women than men are among the poor. The Poverty Trend Analysis in 62 villages found that 76 percent of women fell under the category "poor" in terms of income and resource endowments. Women are discriminated against in intra-household allocation of resources as well, in terms of food, education and health care.

Though women play a major role in the functioning of the household and the economy, they are generally not seen outside the domestic sphere. National statistics have not been able to account for their contribution in the form of domestic work and unpaid labour in family ventures. Although households headed by men are the norm national statistics show that about 8 percent of households are headed by women in Bangladesh. The actual number of female managed households is likely to be much higher than officially reported, nearly 30 percent. The income distribution is more skewed among women headed households and the bottom 20-30 percent of women headed households are among the poorest in Bangladesh. Over the last two decades women have gradually become more visible in the labour force, in development programmes and local institutions. It is worth mentioning that participation rate of females in the labour force is increasing at a faster rate than that of males. Women's role as productive agents whose contribution is crucial to attain a certain standard of living for the family is increasingly being recognized. In addition, the measurement of women's economic activities has been modified to better capture their contribution, as a result of which their participation rates are higher than before. However, women's role should not be conceived in economic terms only. Their status and position should be considered in terms of education, training and job opportunities, income, employment, assets, health, and the role they play in the family and in society. These characteristics are crucial in determining the amount of political power and social prestige a woman is accorded and thus the extent to which she can influence decision-making within the home and in the community.

**Education**

The overall literacy rate of the population (7 years and above) is 32.4. The rate is 38.9 for males compared to 25.5 for females. Male children are still sent to school more frequently and parents are still more likely to spend more on their books made and education than that of girls as it is thought to be an investment in the case of boys who are expected to look after their parents financially in old age. Education for girls is considered as less useful as they are expected to get married and leave their families behind.

Though the enrolment rate for girls has increased significantly to 78 percent, against 88.9 percent for boys, the drop out rate continues to be high. At the primary level completion rate has increased to 60 percent for both boys and girls but it is lower for girls at higher levels. At higher secondary level women's participation reached 25 percent of the total in 1994. At the university level 25 percent students and 14 percent of the teachers are women as of 1994/95. The proportion of women students is significantly less in technical disciplines such as agriculture and engineering which are considered as men's domain. In the technical universities only

9 percent students are women.

**Health and Nutrition**

Due to overall poverty health care receives inadequate resource allocations. At household level too, poverty results in limited expenditure on health care. Women are more disadvantaged than man in terms of access to health care and the quality of nutrition and health care received. Life expectancy is lower by almost a year for women. The household allocation for medical care for women is much lower than that of men (Tk. 18.8 and 24 respectively for women and men in rural areas). Women family members are less likely to receive modern medical care and tend to receive traditional types of care instead. A recent study has found that adult men make up the largest single group to be admitted in hospitals followed by boys. Only 14 percent of births are attended by trained personnel. According to the approach adopted by the health services women's health care is often restricted to their reproductive health and general health of women of all ages is neglected. The nutritional status of girl children, especially of rural girls, is worse than for boys. More than 12 percent of children between the ages of one to five suffer from acute malnutrition as measured by mid-upper arm circumference. For boys the rate is of 11.9 and for girls it is of 13.3 (as of 1992). The prevalence rate for boys in urban areas is 6.5 percent and for girls 10.2 percent. The prevalence rate for boys in rural areas is 12.6 percent for girls 13.7 percent. Biases in parental care, feeding patterns, intra familial food distribution and treatment of illness are all in favour of males. As a result, girl child mortality, malnutrition, morbidity and maternal mortality are high. Women are married at a much lower age than men with an average age gap of 8 years, and the incidence of marriage is highest among women aged 10-19 years. Forty nine percent women in the age group of 15-19 are married. Women's long child bearing span with the first birth at the age of 18 and high birth rate within an average of 4.5 living children aggravates women's nutritional status which is already poor due to inadequate food intake. Studies show that irrespective of income level a large percentage of women suffer from low body weight and height. This contributes to a cycle of high maternal mortality with an MMR of 459 per 100,000, malnutrition and low birth weight babies leading to infant mortality. The Infant Mortality Rate has been reduced from 190/1900 live births in 1080 to 78/1000 at present.

The health situation of urban women is worse than that of women in the rural areas. The urban population living in the slum areas do not have adequate sanitation, water and health facilities which results in poor health. Women and children are the worse sufferers in these places. The increase in rural-urban migration, unemployment and other factors have led to increased health risks for women including vulnerability to STD/HIV/AIDS.

**Population Control and Family Planning**

In the last twenty years Bangladesh has achieved a great deal in this area. Total Fertility Rate (TFR) has fallen to 3.4 with 49 percent of the total population in the reproductive age group. Average age at marriage has increased from 13.5 years in the seventies to 19.9. Contraceptive Prevalence Rate (CPR) has increased to 45 percent. The Planning Commission projections show a population of 137.3 million by the year 2000. However in spite of the considerable achievements of the country various problems still persist. Early age at marriage, lack of opportunities for female education and employment, infant and child mortality rates which are still unacceptably high, and malnutrition persistently influence the high fertility and maternal mortality rates in Bangladesh. The contraceptive prevalence rate has increased to 45 percent.

**Employment**

As regards employment, women in Bangladesh are far behind men. Nearly 43 percent women are involved in agricultural activities but 70 percent of them work as unpaid family labour. The 1991 census indicated that 11 percent of all women were economically active. Labour force participation rates for females stood at 9.9 and 14.1 percent in the Labour Force Surveys (LFS) of 1985-86 and 1990-91 respectively. The use of an extended definition of labour force activities which included a number of expenditure saving activities carried out by women resulted in their participation rate increasing to 61.6, 58.2 and 50.6 in the LFS of 1989. 1990-91 and 1995/96 respectively.

The trends of increasing landlessness and growing numbers of female headed households have subjected women to serious economic pressures. Gradual changes in attitude towards working women are also becoming apparent. An estimated 8 million women, of whom 40 percent live in rural areas, are seeking employment.

The 1995/96 LFS found that 78.8 percent of the women who participated in the labour force were involved in the agriculture and fisheries sectors. Forty percent of the employed women work as unpaid family helpers, 18 percent as day labourers, 25.3 percent as employees and 22.3 percent are self-employed.

Women work harder and longer hours than men. Women's working days range from 14 to 15 hours including child rearing and household management. Women's participation in formal sector employment was negligible until the recent past. Women who were working outside the home were mostly engaged in teaching, medicine and nursing. Due to quota provisions at the entry level, women's participation rate in the public sector has increased to some extent. However, women fill only about 7 percent of the officer ranks, about 10 percent staff positions and only 5 percent at the low level worker positions and they constitute only 9 percent of the total employees. There are still very few at the management or policy making levels. Around 14.14 percent of total recruits into the public service have been women in the last five years.

Women's participation in the industrial sector is largest in the construction industry where many work as manual labourers. In the manufacturing sector, the export oriented industries such as electronics, garments and shrimp processing have attracted women. Rural to urban migration of women in search of jobs is a recent phenomenon. Local textiles, shoes, cosmetics and such other consumable production units have also employed women. The garment manufacturing sub-sector is the largest employer of women. More than three hundred thousand women work in about 2000 garment units and they constitute over 90 percent of the total labour force of the sector. Women's economic participation is greater in the non-formal sector and has increased substantially due to the success of self-employment generating credit programmes run by the government and NGOs.

**Women in Development Plans**

Women are considered as a distinct target group by the national development plans.

The empowerment of women has been emphasized in the latest plans. Among the previous plans, the First Five Year Plan(1973-78) emphasized a welfare oriented approach and focused on the rehabilitation of war affected women and children. Population control was the most important area in which women were considered as beneficiaries. However, their productive role was not emphasized. The Two Year Plan(1978-80) was characterized by a move from welfare to development oriented efforts. Women's development was taken as a central focus. The Second Five Year Plan(1980-85) emphasized undertaking more dynamic and diversified programmes. The major objective was to create an atmosphere for making women's participation in development activities increasingly positive through expanding opportunities for specialized training, skill development, credit and entrepreneurship development programmes. The Third Five Year Plan( 1985-90) built upon the previous plan activities. To achieve the overall integration of women in the development process the Plan had specific objectives to reduce imbalances between the development of men and women.

Within the time span considered by the present report, the Fourth Five Year Plan (FFYP 1990- 95) (11) had as objectives the acceleration of economic growth; poverty alleviation and increasing self reliance. The strategies included integration of sector based planning with group based planning and mainstreaming of women to reduce gender disparities. Development policies with regard to women were placed within the context of a macro economic framework for a multi-sectoral thrust.

The Draft Participatory Perspective Plan (1995-2010) formulated in 1995, though not yet approved as a Plan document, provides a statement of policy. It sets the goal of eliminating all forms of discrimination against women by empowering women and men as equal partners working towards equality, development and peace. Women are to be integrated in the mainstream of development. The targets include the following: the eradication of persistent and increasing burden of poverty on women; equal access to education and training for human resource development; equal access to health care services, elimination of violence against women and girls; access to all forms of productive activities and resources; equal sharing in power and decision making; creation of strong mechanism to promote the advancement of women; promotion of women's human rights; equality in access to, and participation in, the media; equality in the family and society; involvement in environmental protection and conservation; participation as beneficiaries and agents in all sectors of development; participation in all national and international bodies and fora; provision of skill training and credit for self- employment; and survival, development and protection of the girl child.

The following are some of the specific targets :

- Increasing female literacy rate from 24 to 50 by the year 2000;
- Raising adult literacy rate to 62 per cent
- Increasing the enrolment of girls to 94 percent;
- Ensuring health for all women by the year 2000;
- Ensuring adequate nutrition for all women and girls;
- Increasing the share of women's employment from 8 to 30 percent by the year 2000 both in national and foreign service jobs.

National Policy on Women's Advancement: In March 1997 a Policy on Women's Advancement was declared by the Prime Minister which provides a comprehensive framework for women's development in the country.

Fifth Five Year Plan(1997-2002 under formulation): The write up prepared by the Ministry of Women and Children Affairs for the Fifth Five Year Plan outlines a set of comprehensive measures to implement the National Policy for Women's Advancement. The vision of the plan is to guarantee women equal access to opportunities for the realization of the goals of equality, environmentally and socially, sustainable development and people's participation.

The Goals and Objectives of WID during the Fifth Five Year Plan are to:

i) achieve equality between men and women in the sharing of power and decision-making at all levels;

ii) raise awareness and to ensure establishment of women rights recognized nationally and internationally;

iii) establish effective mechanisms with necessary resources and authority at all levels to promote the development of women in all spheres of life;

iv) alleviate poverty and to ensure food security and minimal nutritional requirement of 1,800 k-calorie per person per day for all with emphasis on women;

v) promote economic self-reliance for women including access to economic resources - land, capital and technology;

vi) mainstreaming women's concern in agriculture and rural development, industry and commerce and also in the informal sector;

vii) ensure the visibility and recognition of women's work and to reduce the gender gap in access to information, skill and knowledge about economic opportunities;

viii) raise the rate of female participation in the active labour force (employed) to bring it at par with man;

ix) raise literacy rate of women to about 50 percent and to complete primary education by at least 80 percent of school age children;

x) increase women's full access through the life cycle to health and related services under the goal "Health for All"

xi) eliminate all sorts of violence against women;

xii) eliminate trafficking of women and girl child;

xiii) ensure participation of women in national and international peace negotiations;

xiv) recognize women's role and concern in environmental and natural resources management;

xv) chalk out programmes in the mass media to reflect gender perspective and to focus a positive image of women and girl child; and

xvi) to generate necessary complementary service facilities for the development of women.

The strategies as adopted for the attainment of the objectives are poverty alleviation, public expenditure to address the basic needs of women, support for education, health and legal protection.

The strategic means to implement these include building institutional structure from grassroots to national level, coordination between devleopment policies and activities of various organizations and cooperation between the government and NGOs.

**General Legal Framework Within Which Legal Rights are Protected**

The Parliament and the Ministry of Law, Justice and Parliamentary Affairs are responsible for enacting legal provisions and upholding human rights. The judiciary is responsible for interpretation of laws and judgements and the law enforcing agencies such as the Police are responsible for enforcing the provisions. Individuals whose rights have been violated can seek redress from the judiciary within the context of existing laws.

Special tribunals and courts such as labour courts, administrative tribunals, the Central Cell for the Prevention of Oppression Against Women and Children, respond to specific appeals that fall under their jurisdiction. Certain human rights are protected by the Constitution and these have been elaborated in section

Various provisions of the ILO Conventions have been integrated in the labour laws. In the past various laws have been formulated or amended to ensure equality and protect women's rights. Among these the following may be mentioned:

a) The Muslim Family Laws Ordinance of 1961 which regulates personal matters such as inheritance of property, marriage, divorce, guardianship and custody of children, etc. It sets the minimum age of marriage at 18 for women and 21 for men.

b) The Dowry Prohibition Act of 1980 and its amendment in 1986 has made the custom of dowry an offence, punishable by fine and imprisonment.

c) The Family Court Ordinance of 1985 has established family courts at the district and than levels, to deal with cases relating to marriage and divorce, restitution of conjugal rights, recovery of dower, maintenance and custody of children. Provisions have been made for mediation and quick disposal of cases.

d) The Child Marriage Restraint Act of 1929 provides for a

legal age of marriage and punishment for anyone marrying before that age.

e) The Muslim Marriage and Divorce Registration Act of 1974 provides for the documentation and registration of marriage contracts mentioning the amount of dower.

**National Machineries**

The following national machineries are in existence to further women's advancement:

*Ministry of Women and Children's Affairs*: The Women's Affairs Division which was created in 1976 and upgraded as the Ministry of Women's Affairs in 1978 to deal with the development concerns of women. Bangladesh is one of the few countries in the world having a full fledged Ministry to work for women's advancement. The role of the Ministry includes national policy formulation regarding women, implementation of special programmes for women's development, dealing with matters relating to women's legal and social rights, control and registration of women's voluntary organizations and dealing with international organizations in the field of women's development. The Ministry's role has been expanded to coordinate the WID aspect of different sectors. Recently the Ministry has been given added responsibility for the development and protection of children and their rights.

*National Council For Women's Development (NCWD):* A 44 member National Council for Women's Development (NCWD) has been established consisting of Ministers and Secretaries from several line Ministries, public representatives and eminent individuals with the Prime Minister as Head of the Council.

The responsibilities of NCWD are as follows:

* To ensure women's participation in socio-economic development work, the Council will formulate rules and regulations for the development work of different Ministries, divisions and other agencies and coordinate them;
* The Council will formulate laws, and regulations to ensure women's legal rights and development and to prevent of oppression against women;
* The Council will also take measures to preserve women's interests in all areas in which women are active and

ensure their participation and advancement.

*WID Focal Points in Different Ministries:* Since the Fourth Five Year Plan, all the sectors and Ministries are responsible for incorporating women in development concerns into their development programmes in order to mainstream women's development. Women in Development (WID) Focal Points in 33 Ministries and agencies are responsible for overseeing the concerns of women in the programmes of their respective Ministries. They are responsible for formulating sectoral plans keeping in mind gender concerns, preparing lists of priority projects for women for inclusion in the annual development plans; reviewing and modifying ongoing projects with a view to incorporating adequate gender concerns in the sectoral programmes/projects; ensuring gender sensitive reporting system; collaborating with other sectors and central agencies in order to achieve WID sectoral goals; and monitoring and reporting on their sectoral activities and constraints in achieving these goals.

*Interministerial Coordination and Evaluation Committee*: The National Women's Advancement Policy envisages the establishment of an Interministerial Coordination and Evaluation Committee headed by the Minister for Women and Children's Affairs to monitor the progress of implementation of sectoral WID plans and programmes and submit quarterly progress reports to the NCWD. Various government and non-government women's development organizations and Ministries with WID Focal Points, will be members of this committee.

*Department of Women's Affairs:* The Directorate of Women's Affairs was established in 1976 and was upgraded in 1990 to the Department of Women's Affairs. It functions as the implementing arm of the Ministry of Women and Children Affairs. It operates through its head quarter and field based offices in order to implement the activities and directives of the Ministry. Its activities include awareness raising on women's rights and equality, vocational and technical training in various areas, providing credit facilities and providing legal aid services to women.

*Jatiya Mohila Shangstha (JMS):* Jatiya Mohila Shangstha (JMS) was created in 1976 as the apex national women's organization to further the social, economic, educational and cultural upliftment of women. It has undergone many changes with regard to its activities and character since its inception. It was declared an autonomous organization through an ordinance in 1991 and named as Jatiya Mohila Shangstha. It works under the Ministry of Women and Children Affairs. The main activities it has undertaken are skill development training in weaving, handicrafts, tailoring and motivation for family planning, tree plantation, sanitation and micro-credit operations in selected "Thanas" or Sub-Districts. The programmes are conducted using government granted funds. A unit computer training and a legal aid cell for women have been established.

**Information and Publicity**

The Government is responsible for the dissemination of information on various human rights instruments and the legal provisions on human rights that have been ratified. Various NGOs and human rights groups also undertake specific programmes for raising awareness on this among the public. Efforts in this area have been limited and inadequate so far. Some instruments such as The Convention on the Elimination of All Forms of Discrimination Against Women, Child Rights Convention and the Human Rights Convention have been translated into Bangla by the local UN Offices and NGOs for dissemination among the public.

**Remaining Obstacles Encountered by Women**

The Government of Bangladesh ratified the Convention on the Elimination of All Forms of discriminations Against Women (CEDAW) excluding the Clauses 2, 13(a), 16 (1) (c) and (f) which relate to the personal rights of women such as succession of property, marriage and divorce, guardianship over children etc.

The constitution guarantees equality between men and women in the public sphere. Various discriminatory customs and practices persist, however, which are gradually being addressed and removed through appropriate measures. The present Government is committed to remove these discriminatory provisions. The Constitution allows for Personal Laws in the private sphere which are in some cases discriminatory against women. Unequal provisions in personal laws such as in the case of inheritance, guardianship of children, marriage and divorce contributes to their inferior social, economic political and legal status.

There are problems in implementing existing legal provisions due to women's, as well as men's. ignorance about their legal rights. The substance as well as application of laws puts women in a disadvantaged position with regard to men.

**Obligations to Eliminate Discrimination**

State Parties condemn discrimination against women in all its forms, agree to pursue by all appropriate means and without delay a policy of eliminating discrimination against women and, to this end, undertake:

(a) To embody the principle of the equality of men and women in their national constitutions or other appropriate legislation if not yet incorporated therein and to ensure, through law and other appropriate means, the practical realization of this principle;

(b) To adopt progressive legislative and other measures, including sanctions where appropriate, prohibiting discrimination against women;

(c) To establish legal protection of the rights of women on an equal basis with men and to ensure through competent national tribunals and other public institutions the effective protection of women against any act of discrimination;

(d) To refrain from engaging in any act or practice of discrimination against women and to ensure that public authorities and institutions shall act in conformity with this obligation;

(e) To take all appropriate measures to eliminate discrimination against women by any person, organization or enterprise;

(f) To take all appropriate measures, including legislation, to modify or abolish existing laws, regulations, customs and practices which constitute discrimination against women;

(g) To repeal all national penal provisions which constitute discrimination against women.

**Constitutional Provisions for Women**

The legal status of women in Bangladesh has been

defined in the Constitution. Article 27 States: All citizens are equal before the law and are entitled to equal protection of the law. Article 28 of the Constitution States:

1) The state shall not discriminate against any citizen on grounds only of religion, race, caste, sex or place of birth.
2) Women shall have equal rights with men in all spheres of the State and of public life.
3) No citizen shall, on grounds only of religion, race, caste, sex or place of birth, be subjected to any disability, liability, restriction or condition with regard to access to any place of public entertainment or resort, or admission to any educational institution.
4) Nothing in this Article shall prevent the State from making special provision in favour of women and children or for the advancement of any backward section of the population.

Article 26 of the Constitution States that:

1) All existing laws inconsistent with the fundamental rights shall, to the extent of inconsistency, become void on the commencement of this Constitution.
2) The State shall not make any law inconsistent with any provisions of this Part, and any law so made shall, to the extent of such inconsistency, become void.

As citizens, women also enjoy the following fundamental rights as provided by the Bangladesh Constitution:

* No discrimination against any citizen on grounds of religion, race, caste, sex or place of birth
* equality of opportunity in public employment * right to protection of law
* protection of right to life and personal liberty
* prohibition of forced labour
* safeguards as to arrest and detention
* protection in respect of trial and punishment
* freedom of movement, assembly, association, thought and conscience, speech, profession, occupation and religion
* right to property
* protection of home and correspondence
* enforcement of fundamental rights through courts of law

**Legislative and Other Measures Adopted to Eliminate Discrimination Against Women**

Though the Constitution guarantees equal rights for men

and women in public life it does not extend this to the private sphere where the various personal laws based on religion are recognized. These are discriminatory with regard to various provisions such as marriage and divorce, inheritance, guardianship, etc. The Constitution also recognizes the unequal situation of women in so far as it recognizes the need to make special provisions for them as a specially disadvantaged category. Bangladesh has ratified the Convention on the Elimination of All forms of Discrimination Against Women (CEDAW) with reservations and not accepted it as legally binding yet. Most national laws are already in conformity with the provisions of the Convention. Some reforms/modifications have been made to protect the rights of women.

Certain legislative actions have been taken to protect the interests of women and reduce discrimination. Some of these are through the enactment of new laws and others through modifications of the existing laws and procedures. The legislative measures include reform of family laws, laws on equal pay and employment, protection and expanded political rights. The changes in the national legislation which have taken place during the last two decades have been the result of the ratification of various conventions and the mutually reinforcing developments in international and national laws. Some provisions of the Muslim Personal Laws have been modified but as yet no effective measures have been taken to reform the Hindu personal laws or laws of other minority groups as it was felt that such proposals would not be endorsed by the respective religious/ minority communities.

Within the reporting period a new law the Women and Child Repression (Special Provision) Act of 1995 further increases the punishment for crimes against women. It has been enacted to prevent and punish cruelty to women and children in the form of abuse, injury, or death using corrosive, poisonous or combustive substance or for dowry. It makes provisions for the punishment of kidnapping or abduction of women or children to use them for prostitution or illegal cohabitation, etc. Special Courts have been instituted with Session Judges or Additional Session Judges in each district. It provides for completion of the investigation of such offense within 60 days of the receipt of the "First Information Report"

(FIR) or order for investigation and not to grant bail to the accused during that period. There is also a provision for completion of the trial within 90 days of receipt of the case.

Besides the government has constituted a high powered committee headed by the Minister for Law, Justice and Parliamentary Affairs to examine existing laws and update them to address all forms of discrimination against women.

**Major Obstacles to Implementation**

The protection that is accorded through the civil laws are outweighed by the inequalities reflected in many areas of personal laws governing the life of women. Women's socio-economic status differs from their legal status. The former often determines the latter. Although the Government is determined to take steps to eliminate discrimination against women through legal measures, women cannot even enjoy those rights provided by existing laws due to the lack of enforcement. The disparity between the rights women have by law and what they actually enjoy arises partly from the lack of knowledge of women and men about internationally and nationally recognized womenþs rights and the lack of commitment by the judiciary and law enforcement agencies.

Various procedures make it difficult for women to access and use the judicial system. For example the language used is esoteric, the procedures lengthy and therefore costly and the agencies are often hostile or unsympathetic to women. The proof required to file a case of domestic violence or rape is an obstacle. The lack of birth registration makes the enforcement of the Child Marriage Act is difficult. The lack of a central database on marriage and divorce registrations, or any means of cross-checking such registrations, means that it is virtually impossible to prevent polygamy. Although the Muslim Family Law allows women to inherit, social customs and family pressure often prevent women from claiming their share. Women lack the financial resources required and lack access to lawyers and courts which restricts their recourse to the legal system.

**Reservation of Article 2**

The Government of Bangladesh placed reservation to Articles 13 (a) and 16 (1) (c) which were thought to be in contradiction with Shariah Law derived from the Holy Quran and Sunnah. By deduction the reservation an Article two was placed. All of the reservations are in the process of being reviewed. The Ministry of Women and Children's Affairs constituted an interministerial committee in November 1996 to review the reservations made to the Convention and make recommendations. It has as members from the Ministries of Information, Law, Home Affairs and Women and Children's Affairs. It also has two women lawyers and activists as members. A report has been submitted in February 1997 for consideration to the highest authority.

As mentioned above, the Constitution of the country embodies the principle of equality between women and men and declares that constitutional principles shall take precedence over all other existing laws. The Constitution is the highest law of the land and any law inconsistent with the Constitution is automatically void (Articles 7(2) and 26). Thus all pre-Constitutional laws have to withstand the test of the Constitution's basic principles.

Bangladesh does not have any "Shariah Law" as such. Rather certain provisions are codified into legislation, such as the Muslim Family Law Ordinance and provisions of the Shariah are not immutable but subject to reinterpretation based on the needs of the time. In addition Muslims are not the only population in the country. There is a sizeable non-Muslim population to whom the Shariah is not applicable.

Bangladesh is committed to its international treaty obligations and the guarantees of equality between men and women and of non-discrimination against women contained in the UN Charter, the Universal Declaration of Human Rights and other international instruments.

Various women's organizations have arranged seminars and conferences to discuss the Convention and the justifications for the reservations made. Pre-Beijing a series of regional workshops as well as a national workshop were held by the NGO Preparatory Committee for the NGO Forum.

Besides several training and seminars have also been organized by the CEDAW Forum which brings together various organizations and individuals seeking withdrawal of reservations and full implementation of the Convention. It addition several women's organizations such as Bangladesh Mohila Parishad, Bangladesh Jatiya Mohila Ainjibi Samity, Naripokkho and USHA have been working in this area individually.

**The Development and Advancement of Women**

State Parties shall take in all fields, in particular in the political, social, economic and cultural fields, all appropriate measures, including legislation, to ensure the full development and advancement of women, for the purpose of guaranteeing them the exercise and enjoyment of human rights and fundamental freedoms on a basis of equality with men. Legally women have the same access as men to the political process, social services, health and medical care, education, literacy, development programmes, employment, ownership of property and social welfare.

In certain cases temporary special measures have been formulated to increase womenþs access to these services and programmes. The exercise and enjoyment of human rights and fundamental freedoms by women, on the basis of equality with men, is guaranteed under the Constitution and other relevant laws.

However, in fact, women do not have the same access as men to these rights and freedoms. The situation with regard to political life, education and health is described while discussing articles 7, 10 and 12 respectively. Various kinds of remedial measures have been taken up as a result of which the situation in many sectors is improving. It needs to be stressed that developments or advancements in any one sector are closely related with developments or advancements in other sectors. For example developments in education are important for improvements in political participation or employment.

One of the major obstacles is women's unequal status in the personal sphere which means that the grounds for their participation in the public sphere are also unequal. Women's lower socio-economic status , lower literacy, lesser mobility are all practical obstacles to the exercise of their fundamental rights.

A phenomenon which has emerged recently illustrates the difficulties women have in exercising their rights because of cultural practices and misinterpretation of religion. It is that of extra- judicial procedures whereby village bodies try and punish women for various "offenses" invoking the Shariah and passing judgements or "fatwas". These have used the mechanism of the village "shalish" recognized by law only as a mediation body which requires the consent and presence of both parties to be effective and for its judgements to be recognized. Its mandate is restricted to certain specific items but does not extend to marriage, dissolution of marriage and other such issues covered by the laws of the land. However, there have been instances of these bodies being used to "try" and punish women using religious grounds, in cases of marital dispute, dissolution of marriage and adultery.

The Government has taken staunch measures against such extra-judicial practices, bringing those responsible to justice.

Various measures have been taken to enhance the status of women with regard to political participation and participation in social, economic and cultural life. Unfortunately, in the past these policies and measures were taken on behalf of women without their full participation. At present, however, their participation is being sought. For example many women activists and womenþs organizations are participating in the various debates and putting forward various proposals in the discussions on reserving a certain number of seats in the National Parliament for women.

A National Policy on Women's Advancement was approved by the National Council for Women's Development (NCWD) in February 1997 and declared by the Prime Minister on March 08, 1997. Its main objectives are as follows:

* Establish equality between men and women in all spheres;
* Eliminate all forms of discrimination against women and girls;
* Establish women's human rights;
* Develop women as human resource;
* Recognize women's contribution in social and economic spheres;
* Eliminate poverty among women;
* Establish equality between men and women in administration, politics, education, games, sports and all

other socio-economic spheres;
* Eliminate all forms of oppression against women and girls;
* Ensure empowerment of women in the fields of politics, administration and the economy;
* Develop appropriate technology for women;
* Ensure adequate health and nutrition for women;
* Provide housing and shelter to women;
* Create positive images of women in the media;
* Take special measures for women in especially disadvantaged situations.

With regard to the monitoring of the implementation of the various policies, programmes and laws, the National Council for Women's Development and the Interministerial Coordination and Evaluation Committee provide institutional mechanisms through which reputed individuals and various women's organizations can participate.

**Temporary Special Measures: 1**

Adoption by the State Parties of temporary special measures aimed at accelerating de facto equality between men and women shall not be considered discrimination as defined in the present Convention, but shall in no way entail as a consequence the maintenance of unequal or separate standards; these measures shall be discontinued when the objectives of equality of opportunity and treatment have been achieved. Adoption by State Parties of special measures, including those measures contained in the present Convention, aimed at protecting maternity shall not be considered discriminatory. *Policies:* Article 28 of the Constitution states that the State may make special provisions for women and children, recognizing that they are specially disadvantaged. Official policy also aims to accelerate attainment of de facto equality of women and men. The Fourth Five Year Plan (1990-95) integrated womenþs development into a macro-framework in order to formulate a multi-sectoral thrust to bring women into the mainstream of development. The Draft Perspective Plan formulated for the period 1995 to 2005 also put special emphasis on women's development.

*National Machinery:* Separate national machinery for the advancement of women has been set up. The Ministry of

Women's Affairs was established in 1978 and the Department of Women's Affairs was established in 1984. WID Focal Points have been identified in 33 Ministries and agencies as a means of inter-ministerial coordination on women's issues to ensure the mainstreaming of women's concerns into all sectoral projects, programmes and policy statements. The mechanism is being coordinated by the Ministry of Women and Children's Affairs. A National Council for Women's Development was established in 1995 with the Prime Minister as the chair, to act as the highest policy making body and monitor and oversee women related activities in the various sectors. Its first meeting was held on February 18, 1997 to discuss and approve the National Policy for Women's Advancement. An Interministerial Coordination and Evaluation Committee headed by the Minister for Women and Children's Affairs has been set-up to monitor the progress of implementation of sectoral WID plans and programmes.

*Political Representation:* In order to ensure women's representation in the Parliament a special provision has been made for 30 seats for women in addition to the 300 seats of the Parliament as provided by the Constitution. This special provision is valid up to 1999. Women are to be elected to those thirty seats by the other directly elected Members of Parliament.

Women are also eligible to contest through direct elections for the other unreserved seats. Such provisions have also been made in local government bodies. The Municipal Corporation have provisions for three women Ward Commissioners out of a total of twelve members. The four city corporations have 38 women members.

The women members are to be nominated and selected by the elected members. The Union Parishad or Council, the lowest administrative unit also has a provision for three women members out of a total membership of 12. Here too, the women members are nominated and elected by the other directly elected members.

The impact of these measures has yet to be felt in terms of increased representation of women in the directly elected seats.

*Decade of the Girl Child:* In recognition of the discrimination faced by women throughout their life-cycle and beginning as girls, the South Asian Association for Regional Cooperation (SAARC) has declared the 1990s as the Decade of the Girl Child in the Male Summit in 1990. Each country formulated Decade Plans for the advancement of girls.

The Bangladesh Decade Plan, "Samata" (Equality) was prepared by multiple partners dealing with children's issues and is both a set of programme objectives and an advocacy tool for improving the status of the girl child. It has the following major goals:

* Reduction of Infant Mortality Rate to 50 per 1000 live births by the year 2000 while eliminating gender disparity in rates.
* Reduction of Under-5 mortality rate to 70 per 1000 live births by the year 2000 while eliminating gender disparity in rates.
* Education of Maternal Mortality rate to 3.5 per 1000 live births by the year 2000 while raising female age at marriage to 18, delaying first pregnancy to 20 and increasing CPR to 50 by the year 2000.
* Reduction of severe and moderate malnutrition by half between 1990 and 2000.
* Increasing access to safe water for drinking and other purposes from 80 percent in 1990 to universal coverage by 1995 and maintaining the level.
* Increasing the availability of, and access to, sanitary latrines from 6 percent in 1990 to 35 percent in 1995 and 80 percent in 2000.
* Increasing access to, and enrolment in, primary education, to 95 percent by 2000, covering not less than 75 percent of girls by 1995 and 90 percent by 2000. Increasing the primary school completion rate for girls to atleast 65 percent by 2000. Efforts will be made to reach the global goal of 80 percent completion rate by 2000.

  Progressive and rapid increase in social support services and legal measures to prevent and protect girls from being exploited or abused, with special focus on children in especially difficult circumstances. Accelerated efforts will be made to reduce and steadily eliminate child labour in accordance with the Colombo Resolution on Children (SAARC, 1992).

  *Special Programmes:* There are a number of special women

targeted projects in each sector: health, education, agriculture, etc. Various measures have been taken in education to increase the enrolment and retention of girls. Their impact is gradually being felt in increasing enrolment and retention rates in primary schools. The special health risks of women related to child birth have been recognized and special intensive and coordinated programmes are being undertaken to reduce maternal and infant mortality rates. Here, too, the impacts are gradually being felt.

Even among the relief and rehabilitation programmes, recognizing the special vulnerability of women to poverty, three of the programmes are specifically targeted toward women: the Vulnerable Group Development Programme with 399,091 beneficiaries delivers a monthly ration of 31.25 kilograms of wheat per person to especially vulnerable and destitute women (women of female headed households who are lactating or with children); the Rural Maintenance Programme, a monetized food aid programme, which employs poor women for the maintenance of rural roads, and the Post Monsoon Rehabilitation.

**Maternity Leave and Day-care**

In the formal sector maternity leave is allowed for three months twice in the working life of a woman. In the private and non formal sector this has not yet been ensured although most ILO conventions in this respect have been ratified. Labour laws provide for maternity leave and also for child care facilities where more than fifty women are employed. Women are exempted from night work in factories under the labour law. In reality very few women enjoy these benefits. Pilot programmes by certain NGOs have been started to establish day-care centres for women garment workers in the factories in collaboration with the employers. Another new and innovative programme is to set up schools for the child workers who have been removed from the garment factories. This programme is being carried out with the garment manufacturers, the Bangladesh Garment Manufacturers and Exporters Association (BGMEA), the Government, ILO and UNICEF in collaboration with NGOs.

**Public Sector Employment**

A quota system has been instituted for recruitment to

Government service which is 10 percent for officers and 15 percent for other categories. In education, in order to increase the proportion of women primary school teachers 60 percent of all new recruits are supposed to be women. However, these quotas are not being fulfilled with the result that only 7 percent of Government employees are women at the officer level and 9 percent at other levels. New recruitment being limited, the impact of recruitment quotas in eliminating the gender gap in total employment is also limited.

Very recently the Government has taken a decision to undertake a special programme for the appointment of women to senior administrative/management posts of Deputy Secretary and Joint Secretary. In addition positive discrimination is made for women government servants while allocating staff housing. Though various special measures are in place, enforcement measures could not be ensured in all areas and the Government is committed to develop mechanisms for monitoring of the impact and progress achieved.

**Sex Roles and Stereotyping**

State parties shall take all appropriate measures:

(a) To modify the social and cultural patterns of conduct of men and women, with a view to achieving the elimination of prejudices and customary and all other practices which are based on the idea of the inferiority of the superiority of either of the sexes or on stereotyped roles for men and women;

(b) To ensure that family education includes a proper understanding of maternity as a social function and the recognition of the common responsibility of men and women in the upbringing and development of their children, it being understood that the interest of children is the primordial consideration in all cases.

Despite efforts to achieve legal and de facto equality, true advancement toward equality requires fundamental social and cultural change. Social and cultural patterns that lead to discrimination and stereotyped roles for women need to be changed. Interpersonal relationships between men and women and practices based on ideas of superiority and inferiority of one sex in relation to another and sex-stereotyping need to be addressed. To this end the recognition of family life as a vital area, maternity as a social function and the need for shared responsibility of men and women in the upbringing of children, needs to be stressed. Social expectations of the roles to be played by women are still very traditional, giving importance to child rearing and household management. The practice of seclusion ('purdah') although changing because of many practical reasons, is still socially valued. The increasing practice of dowry which is a recent phenomena is one of the worst forms of discrimination against women. It is not condoned by Islam but is a social custom.

The definitions of women's work makes them invisible in national statistics. Their employment rates are shown as 50.6. It is only with revised definitions of agricultural work which have taken into consideration the tasks performed by women that the recent Labour Force Survey has shown an increased percentage of women active in agriculture. Women are generally not recognized as farmers. It has been one of the demands of some womenþs organizations to accord them this status. The increased incidence of poverty, rising economic aspirations and increasing urbanization are phenomena contributing to the breaking of traditional values and changing social structures, forcing women to come out of seclusion. This has helped reduce the prejudices against women's working outside the home.

The social stereotypes of the roles expected of men and women are naturally reflected in the media and in the educational curriculum. Apart from the Film Censor Board there are no mechanisms to control the images of women shown in the media. In view of the fundamental right of freedom of expression, the issue of external control over the media is a debatable one. In the age of globalization and the importance of international media such as cable networks and satellite television, the effectiveness of controls by any one country is limited. It is therefore necessary to sensitize media workers of the implications of their work and encourage the development of self-regulatory mechanisms by which the media would itself formulate a code of ethics which would include issues such as the portrayal of women, women in advertising and reporting on cases of violence against women.

Various government agencies and NGOs are using the national media to produce and broadcast promotional materials for the general public and women about health, nutrition, sanitation, education, sending children to school, homestead gardening, etc. However, sometimes these very messages reinforce certain other stereotypes of women's roles. For instance mothers' responsibility in feeding and educating children and women's role in agriculture as confined to vegetable gardening. The realization that educational curricula contribute to sex stereotyping has gradually gained acceptance. Various measures have been taken to revise the educational curricula. Girls and boys are now given the option of taking up Home Economics or Agricultural Studies in Secondary Schools, whereas before Home Economics was for girls and Agricultural Studies for boys. The process of removing sex stereotyping the curricula is not yet complete but will need to continue as an on-going process.

As a complementary measure, teachers will need to be sensitized on these issues. As part of the mobilization and awareness raising programmes on the issues of the Girl Child a special communications initiative, "Meena" has been launched. It focuses on the positive life process of a South Asian girl. Meena, an animation series, is screened on TV, cinema halls and by mobile film units of the Mass Communications Department. The objective is to spread positive messages and help enhance the social worth of the girl child all over the country. Various government training institutions such as the Academy for Planning and Development, Public Administration Training Centre and various NGOs have included gender and WID concerns in their training programmes. Gender training is in the process of becoming institutionalized. This will be an important means of changing attitudes toward women within the Government and thereby changing the approach of various policies, programmes and projects.

Mobilization against violence against women and against the practice of giving and receiving dowry is gaining momentum. The various legal measures taken do not always result in increased punishments or convictions but they contribute towards raising awareness that such violence is against women's human rights and a criminal offense. The Women and Child Repression (Special Provision) Act of 1995 is one such law. The Ministry of Home has set up four women's investigation cells in four police stations, staffed by women police officers. These cells have been set up to facilitate women's access to the Police. They receive complaints and carry out investigations. Based on a review of the performance of these cells the decision whether to expand their number will be taken.

The Department of Women's Affairs has established a Cell Against Violence Against Women. It provides legal counselling and assistance to both civil and criminal cases related to violence against women. In 1996 it death with 83 cases of acid throwing; 1415 cases of rape; 1664 cases of physical assault; 138 cases of trafficking; 85 cases of procurement of women for illicit reasons; 594 cases of dowry; 115 cases of maintenance. 1539 cases of suicide, a total of 5933 cases in all. In 1995/96 the Dhaka unit received 1176 cases. It carried out 550 cases of restoration of family relations, 363 cases of procuration of maintenance and dower money of an amount of 688,280 Takas. Legal counselling was provided in 185 cases. Twenty-nine cases were filed in court. Ninety-one cases were sent to other agencies.

In the districts and thanas which have officers of the Department of Women's Affairs, committees against violence against women have been set up. They are chaired by the administrative head of the district or thana (Deputy Commissioner or Thana Nirbahi Officer) and the Women's Affairs Officer is the Member Secretary. Various cases and complaints are sent to these committees. Thana level committees help in mediation, provide counselling and, if necessary, assist with legal proceedings.

The Ministry of Women and Children's Affairs is preparing an integrated project addressing violence against women. Its objectives include the following:

* To improve the quality of services and the effectiveness of investigative, enforcement, judicial medico-legal, health, custodial and other administrative agencies responsible for dealing with various aspects of crimes and violence against women.

* To provide women better access to the criminal and legal justice systems of the country, with particular emphasis on the access of poor women.
* To create general awareness of the issues of crimes and violence against women through public education campaigns.

The Government has become increasingly more conscious of various violence related issues such as custodial rape, rape by members of law enforcement agencies and violence at community level by extra-judicial means through misinterpretation of religion and misuse of local arbitration bodies.

Several such cases were taken up by various women's organizations and human rights groups, around which they organized rallies, processions and press conferences to mobilize public opinion. In some cases the Government has formed enquiry committees. In other cases the issues and incidents have also come up for Parliamentary debate.

**Suppression of the Exploitation of Women**

State Parties shall take all appropriate measures, including legislation, to suppress all forms of traffic in women and exploitation of prostitution of women.

**Trafficking**

Although the phenomenon of trafficking is not a new one its scope seems to be increasing. Women are experiencing dramatic changes in their life due to increasing landlessness and poverty. Their vulnerability often makes them fall prey to exploitation and become victims of trafficking and prostitution. A non-government source reports that about 200,000 women and children have been trafficked to the Middle East in the last 20 years.

Different human rights activists and agencies estimate 200-400 young women and children are smuggled out every month, most of them form Bangladesh to Pakiśtán. Another women lawyers' association estimates that on an average, 4500 women and children from Bangladesh are being trafficked to Pakistan each year and atleast 200,000 women have been trafficked to Pakistan over the last 10 years.

It is estimated by the Indian Social Welfare Board that

there are 500,000 foreign prostitutes in India of whom about 1 percent are from Bangladesh and 2.7% of prostitutes in Calcutta are from Bangladesh. Trafficking is carried out by regional gangs who are well organized and who have links with the various law enforcing agencies, which is why only a very small percentage of the traffickers are caught or the victims recovered. The Government is aware of the problem of trafficking and has taken up measures to prevent it. One such measure is the strengthening of border posts. However, the sheer length of Bangladesh's border with India and Burma makes it impossible to prevent people crossing the borders.

Another measure is the strengthening of legislation and increasing punishments for trafficking. Legal Measures: The Penal Code of 1860 contains provisions for kidnapping, which in general covers trafficking also. Inspite of there being provisions in the Penal Code, these were not being effective in stopping trafficking because of various implementation problems. In 1983 a new Ordinance, the Cruelty to Women (Deterrent Punishment) Ordinance was promulgated. It replaced the relevant sections of the Penal Code. This law increased the punishment to life imprisonment and death penalty for kidnapping or abducting women, trafficking of women and children, attempt to cause death, acid throwing, rape etc.

The Anti-terrorism Ordinance, 1992 provided for punishment of all types of terrorism including harassing women and abducting children and women. This Ordinance was repealed in 1994 due to various problems. The Suppression of Immoral Trafficking Act, 1993 provides for punishment for forcing a girl into prostitution. Abetment by having custody or charge of the girls is also a crime.

Section 11 of the Act prohibits the detention of any female child under the age of 18 against her will in any house, room or places in which prostitution is carried out. The section provides a penalty of maximum three years of imprisonment or fine or both. In 1995 another law, the Woman and Child Repression (Special Provisions) Act 1995 was enacted. It provides for capital punishment to offenders. It debars the granting of bail to persons accused of heinous offenses against women and children. The penalty imposed in section 8 of this act for trafficking and associated offenses is life imprisonment and fine.

Section 9 stipulates a penalty of 10 years with a minimum of 7 years imprisonment for abduction to commit immoral act on women and children. This Act provides for the setting up of separate courts to try cases coming under it, one in each district. So far ten such courts have been established. It is proposed to review their performance and effectiveness before setting up the courts in other districts. However, although laws against trafficking exist, their implementation remains weak. Although the new laws have increased penalties their application has certain technical problems which are in the process of being identified. There is scope for misapplication and harassment of innocent persons. The law enforcing authorities and the judiciary need to be better sensitized about the issues involved. There is a need for stronger action against members of law enforcing authorities who are themselves involved in trafficking.

Regional cooperation is essential to coordinate legal and administrative measures and procedures. Information needs to be shared and extradition of offenders allowed. Victims are sometimes charged with prostitution or immoral behaviour and put in jail. The repatriation of Bangladeshi women trafficked abroad needs to be facilitated. Programmes: Presently measures for the rehabilitation of repatriated victims are limited. Necessary shelters and homes are inadequate within the Government or with NGOs. Programmes are being designed in collaboration with NGOs for the necessary social rehabilitation and reintegration of victims. There are discussions going on presently about the Ministry of Women and Children's Affairs undertaking a project to address the issue of trafficking.

The following activities are envisaged:

* *Situation analysis*:

- preparation of a comprehensive report on child trafficking
- developing a data base on child trafficking

* *Awareness raising for prevention of child trafficking:*

- materials and techniques designed, developed and disseminated

- child trafficking issues incorporated into educational curricula
- networking with NGOs

* *Capacity building of law enforcement agencies.*

* *Rescue, repatriation, rehabilitation and reintegration:*

- effective rescue system developed
- child friendly repatriation process established
- comprehensive rehabilitation and repatriation programmes established

The programme is to be multi-sectoral involving various ministries. An inter-ministerial steering committee will be formed headed by the Minister of the Ministry of Women's Affairs with NGO representation. District level coordination committees will be set-up.

**NGO Mobilization**

At a recently held workshop on child trafficking organized by the Bangladesh Shishu Adhikar Forum in December, 1996 a South-East Asian and a National Action Plan were prepared for NGOs active in the area of trafficking. It was decided to undertake networking and training on databases/information and experience sharing by a Core Group with representatives from Nepal, Pakistan, India and Bangladesh.

The first meeting of the regional Core Group will take place in March 1997 and training is to be arranged between August and December, 1997. The Bangladesh National Plan focuses on legal protection through implementation of existing laws; awareness raising on trafficking; awareness raising and training on laws related to trafficking. It is proposed that law enforcing agencies in collaboration with NGOs mobilize the community through local government bodies, educational institutions, religious institutions and at the national level through the media.

**Prostitution**

Although in most cases trafficking is for prostitution or leads to prostitution, prostitution within the country needs to be discussed separately. There are no statistics on the numbers of prostitutes. The Bangladesh Bureau of Statistics enumerates them as "destitutes" and does not recognize prostitution as an occupation. The Constitution states that "the State shall adopt effective measures to prevent prostitution and gambling". There are laws against forcing anyone into prostitution or into "immoral acts" (Penal Code 72, 73, 74). Soliciting is also against the law (Criminal Procedure Code). However there are no laws against a person of 18 or above engaging in sexual activity in exchange for money. It is sufficient for a prostitute to have an affidavit delivered by a magistrate stating that she is above 18 for her not to be arrested by the Police. That does not preclude harassment and being asked for bribes.

Prostitution is therefore technically neither legal nor illegal but exists in a gap in the law, as in many countries. Therefore prostitutes do not have any legal protection, nor can the State take any legal measures against them. As citizens they can demand the same fundamental rights from the State, such as the right to protection and security, the right to shelter and to basic amenities.

While laws relating to violence against women, including rape, apply equally to prostitutes, in practice they are discriminated against as they will be classified as 'habituated' to sexual intercourse and proof will be considered to be harder to give/accept. Prostitutes are often subjected to harassment and violence from the Police who are theoretically supposed to protect their rights.

There is need for greater public awareness about forced prostitution, among the general public and in particular among the law enforcing agencies and the judiciary. Unless they are treated as full human being with the same rights and privileges as others, it will not be possible to provide them with any protection or ensure fulfillment of their rights.

# Bibliography


Amin, Sajeda, "The Poverty-Purdah Trap in Rural Bangladesh: Implications for Women Roles in the Family", *Working Paper* No.75. Research Division, The Population Council, New York, 1995.

Asian Development Bank (ADB), Bangladesh Annual Economic Update 1997, Economic Performance, Policy Issues and Priority Reforms. Dhaka, 1997.

Bangladesh Institute of Development Studies, Survey on Employment and Occupational Mobility Among Women in Manufacturing Industries of Dhaka City. Dhaka: BIDS, 1993.

Begum, Ferdousi Sultana, *Role of Donor Agencies in Institutionalizing GAD Policies (in Bengali), in Gender and Development: A Special Issue on Policy, Strategy and Experience in Bangladesh,* Dhaka: Gender Trainers Core Group, 1998.

Biswanath, Savitri, et al, "Poverty and Gender: An Analysis for Action Gender in Development", Monograph Series No.2. UNDP, 1996.

Hashemi, M. Syed, et al., Rural Credit Programs and Women's Empowerment in Bangladesh in World Development. Vol. 24, No. 4, pp. 635-653, 1994.

Hossain, Hameeda, et al., No Better Option? Industrial Women Workers in Bangladesh, Dhaka: University Press Limited, 1990.

Islam, Nazrul, Addressing the Urban Poverty Agenda in Bangladesh. Dhaka: University Press Limited, 1995.

Khandker, Shahidur, R., Fighting Poverty with Micro Credit: Experience of the Grameen Bank and Other Programs in Bangladesh. World Bank, Washington, D.C.,1995.

Mahmud, Simeen, Women and Employment in Bangladesh, Research Report No. 127. BIDS, Dhaka, 1990.

_____________, *The Structural Adjustment Program in Bangladesh Implications for Women in Poverty*, BIDS, Dhaka, 1996.

Rahman, Atiq, A Critical Review of the Poverty Situation in Bangladesh in the Eighties, Research Report No. 67, Vol. 1. BIDS, Dhaka, 1988.

Selim, Rukh Gu., Poor Women, NGO Credit, Employment and Poverty in Rural Bangladesh, Working Paper, McGill University, 1995.

Sen, Gita, et al., Poverty, Economic Growth and Gender Equity: The Asian and Pacific Experience. Kuala Lumpur: Asian and Pacific Development Centre, 1995.

United Nations Development Programme, Report on Human Development in Bangladesh, Dhaka: UNDP,1996.

World Bank, Partnership in Development: The World Bank Assistance to Bangladesh. Dhaka Office: World Bank, 1998.

# Index